W9-BCE-954

Language
and Speech

Language and Speech

George A. Miller
Princeton University

W. H. Freeman and Company
San Francisco

Acknowledgments

p. 25   I. Tattersall and N. Eldredge, "Fact, theory, and fantasy in human paleontology," *American Scientist 65*, March 1977. Reprinted by permission of *American Scientist*, journal of Sigma Xi, The Scientific Research Society.

p. 67   P. C. Delattre, A. M. Liberman and F. S. Cooper, "Acoustic loci and transitional cues for consonants," *Journal of the Acoustical Society of America*, Vol. 27, 1955. © 1955 by the Acoustical Society of America.

p. 68   A. M. Liberman, "Some characteristics of perception in the speech mode," in Perception and Its Disorders, *Proceedings of the Association for Research in Nervous and Mental Disease*, Vol. 48. © 1970 by the Association for Research in Nervous and Mental Disease.

p. 69   L. Lisker and A. Abramson, "The voicing dimension: Some experiments in comparative phonetics," *Proceedings of the Sixth International Congress of Phonetic Sciences*, Prague. © 1970 Academia, Publishing House of the Czechoslovak Academy of Sciences.

p. 107   C. E. Shannon, "Prediction and entropy in printed English," *Bell System Technical Journal*, No. 30. © 1951 by the American Telephone and Telegraph Company.

p. 118   Roger Brown, *A First Language: The Early Stages*, Harvard University Press. © 1973 by the President and Fellows of Harvard College.

Illustration Credits

Albert E. Miller   pp. 6–8, 24, 25
Carol Donner   pp. 15, 28–30, 46
Adolf E. Brotman   p. 18

Dana Burns   pp. 20, 27, 33, 41–43, 45, 57, 62, 63, 67–133
Laszlo Kubinyi   p. 38
Alan D. Iselin   pp. 44, 58

Library of Congress Cataloging in Publication Data

Miller, George Armitage, 1920-
      Language and speech.

      Bibliography: p.
      Includes index.
      1. Psycholinguistics. I. Title.
BF455.M593   001.54   80-27018
ISBN   0-7167-1297-0
ISBN   0-7167-1298-9 (pbk.)

Copyright © 1981 by W. H. Freeman and Company

No part of this book may be reproduced by any mechanical, photographic, or electronic process, or in the form of a phonographic recording, nor may it be stored in a retrieval system, transmitted, or otherwise copied for public or private use, without written permission from the publisher.

Printed in the United States of America

1 2 3 4 5 6 7 8 9

BF
455
.M593

Contents

123800

Preface

Time was when the study of language was the study of languages, when those who studied them were humanistic scholars and knowing the languages was less important than understanding the consequential texts that had been written in them. Such scholarship is still alive and well in the great centers of learning, but it is not the subject of this book.

Here we are concerned with a much younger discipline, the science of language, which grew in part from the humanistic study of languages, but which has many other roots. The modern science of language draws on the social and behavioral sciences—on anthropology and psychology especially—and on the preoccupation with symbolic systems that has characterized so much twentieth century philosophy. It also incorporates parts of the biological sciences—in particular those that contribute to a description of the neurophysiological mechanisms involved in producing and hearing speech, and those branches of comparative biology that enable us to compare linguistics with other systems of animal communication. And it has benefitted from the enormous growth of communication technologies, which have not only contributed essential instrumentation, but have provided a continuing source of practical applications and opportunities.

In an age when new branches of science are splitting off more rapidly than anyone can record, this convergence of many different fields in the science of language is a noteworthy exception. No doubt it reflects the importance of language, and the realization that it is too complex to understand from any single point of view. Language is everywhere, like the air we breathe, and serves a million human purposes.

All of which makes the science of language exciting work. There are certain problems, however, when one tries to share this excitement with others. The range of questions, the variety of methods, the diversity of presuppositions make selection essential, but how is one to find a door that opens onto the whole field? With so many different sub-specializations, how can one convey the larger sense of a coherent, interrelated intellectual enterprise?

In this book I have taken the biological basis of human language as my narrative thread. Other threads could be chosen, but it seems to me that the true miracle of language is that such a thing as language actually exists. When you ask how such an improbability could occur, you are asking how it evolved, and that is a biological question. Unfortunately, we can never know exactly how it evolved, but the fact that evolution shaped humans into linguistic creatures is undeniable, and has important implications for almost every branch of the science of language.

A focus on the biological side of language thus provided a basis for selecting particular topics from a wide range of different approaches, yet imposed a common theme that I hope will suggest the underlying coherence of the field. How well this strategy has succeeded I must leave for the reader to judge.

•   •   •

I would like to express my indebtedness to the many colleagues whose ideas and research I have appropriated in these pages, without explicit citations. Workers in the field will recognize the true sources; readers coming to the field for the first time will not be interested; readers who become interested can track the sources down from the Guide to Further Reading.

I also wish to express my gratitude to Katherine James Miller for assistance in every phase of preparing the manuscript for publication and to Donna Kwilosz Lyons for preparing the Index.

Harvard University Press has kindly given me permission to excerpt material from *A First Language: The Early Stages,* by Roger Brown. Copyright 1973 by the President and Fellows of Harvard College.

January 1981   George A. Miller

Language
and Speech

1

Uniquely Human

Organic evolution has taken many strange turns. Who can say which was most surprising? Every living thing along its random walk was an incredible achievement in biological engineering.

Nonetheless, anthropocentric arrogance has always placed one fruit of evolution above all others, often so far above that it seemed a special gift to humankind from whatever gods we worshiped. Even scientists able to conceive of a cow as a biochemical machine have boggled at the incredible gift of language.

Why? Because the symbolic abilities that underlie human language made possible another mode of biological adaptation, one that is not transmitted genetically but supplements the genetically transmitted adaptations of organic evolution. The human capacity for language made human culture possible, and culture, with all its social, artistic, technological and scientific innovations, set *Homo sapiens* apart from all other animals. It enabled this big-brained, loudmouthed, featherless biped to overrun the earth—to understand and, through understanding, to control the adaptive process itself. Little wonder that the gift of language has so often been seen as nothing less than a divine miracle.

Max Black, a logician and philosopher at Cornell University, once commented that to insist on the importance of language is like battering at an open door. "But," he added, "there are times when it is necessary not to flinch from the obvious." The 20th century has certainly not flinched from

1

recognizing the importance of language. Ours has been an age of intense, almost morbid interest in language—in symbols, meaning, communication. In a time of growing apprehension that modern culture is headed for disaster, preoccupation with the human faculty that makes culture possible is not inappropriate.

Language can be studied from many points of view. The special responsibility of the scientific perspective is to say what language is, to describe it as a natural phenomenon and to explain its form and function. But anything as complicated as human language does not reveal its secrets easily, even to science.

Scientific progress has been most rapid in the study of speech, the tangible manifestation of language. This progress is attributable to the growth of communication technology and the consequent availability of acoustic, electronic, radiographic and computational instruments for analyzing and synthesizing speech signals. The science of linguistics has also flourished. Theoretical linguistics, borrowing conceptual tools sharpened by logicians for the analysis of symbolic systems, has emerged as one of the most rigorous of the social sciences; anthropological linguistics has now accumulated a sample of the world's languages broad enough to support serious analysis of their differences and similarities. Both speech science and linguistic theory have contributed to psychological studies of language and its implications for human perception, learning, thought and action. The scientific preoccupation with language has been both wide and deep.

But much is still not understood. At first each line of work went its own way, but as each sphere of knowledge enlarged, it became increasingly clear that certain common problems cut across disciplinary boundaries. Central to those shared concerns is the need to understand better the human faculty itself—to understand the biological foundations for the human capacities of speech, language and symbolic thought.

This book tries to explain how concern with the underlying capacity for language has arisen in different research contexts and what each approach has contributed to our understanding of this uniquely human capacity. It is hoped that a reader will gain from these pages not only a glimpse of how the methods of science have been applied but also a deeper understanding of and respect for the incredible gift of language.

Let us begin by considering language as a form of knowledge and the human capacity for language as the capacity to acquire and use that kind of knowledge.

We say "Mary knows Russian" or "John knows English and French but not Japanese." What does it mean to know a language? What kind of knowledge is this?

In everyday speech, a person who is said to know a language is able to speak it, to be understood by others who speak it and to understand what they say in reply. Knowing a language is knowing how to use the language.

At the outset, therefore, we must distinguish two kinds of knowing: knowing *how* and knowing *that*. People are said to know how if they possess a certain ability; they are said to know that if they possess factual information. If you are able to read these lines, you already know how to use English, but you may or may not have much factual information about English or about your ability to use it.

A person who knows English will say such things as "She is happy" and "They are happy" and will not say such things as "She are happy" and "They is happy." Saying the first two and avoiding the second two is part of knowing how to speak English. A person who knows how to speak English, however, may not know that the second two examples are wrong because they violate the grammatical rule of number agreement: the subject and the verb of any sentence must agree in number, singular or plural. Knowing this rule is a matter of knowing that.

It is possible to know that without knowing how. You could know that the rule of number agreement also holds in German without knowing how to speak German. In one sense, people who know how to speak English must know the rule of number agreement, because their speech conforms to it, but in another sense, they do not know it if they cannot tell you the rule they are conforming to. That is the difference between knowing how and knowing that.

Fortunately, the thats are easier to learn when you already know the hows. Because you already know how to use English, I will build on that knowledge. What I will say about English, however, could be said of most other languages, with appropriate substitutions, because I am bringing out general principles, principles that reflect the most universal facts about how human beings can learn and use languages. It is a fundamental assumption that there can be a general theory of language, a theory that is more than a collection of descriptions of particular languages, a theory that can teach us something about the underlying human capacity for language.

Consider this fact: every human society has some form of language. We could not make such a statement if we were not able to recognize languages, and we would not be able to recognize a form of social interaction as a language unless all languages had something in common. In fact, all languages of the world have a great deal in common. They have so much in common that it is possible to teach students general methods for recording and analyzing exotic languages that no linguist or anthropologist has ever studied: all human languages are spoken, and there are general methods for reducing them to writing; all human languages have words, or wordlike segments, and there are general methods for compiling them in dictionaries; all human languages use sentences, and there are general methods for stating their grammatical rules. That such similar forms of communication could arise independently in every human group, however isolated, suggests there is a biological basis for the human capacity for language.

Consider this fact: there are thousands of different languages in the world. Exactly how many there are depends on how you count; some linguists would say there are two languages where other linguists would say there are two dialects of a single language. But, however you count, there are thousands of different languages. This great variation reflects the conventional nature of linguistic knowledge.

Conventional knowledge, such as knowing that in the United States people drive on the right side of the road, is knowledge of what people have agreed to. It does not matter which side of the road people drive on, as long as everybody agrees to drive on the same side. A convention is clearly to everyone's advantage just as long as everyone agrees to it. Thus, agreeing to call a chair "chair" is a matter of social convention. In other languages, chairs are called by other names. What name is used does not matter as long as everyone agrees to use the same one.

In the *Cratylus*, the earliest known attempt to discuss the origin of language, Socrates presented two views that have competed ever since. One view is that language originated from the nature of things, the other that it originated in custom or convention. Both views have survived because both are correct, though not, perhaps, in the way or for the reasons Socrates and his friends supposed. Today we would say that language originated from the biological nature of human beings, but it is part of our biological nature that we are free to adopt elaborate linguistic conventions. The basic biological capacity for language can be realized in an indefinitely large number of ways.

The least freedom is available for the sounds of a language—the component of language that is called its *phonology*—because the human vocal tract is much the same the world over. There are only a limited number of ways of using it to make communicable noises. The greatest freedom is available for the words of a language—the component of language that is called its *lexicon*—because different societies can decide that different things are worth naming and can adopt whatever phonological forms they can agree on to serve as names. The rules for forming sentences—the component of language that is called its *syntax*—seem to be intermediate. The variety of syntactic rules is apparently more limited than we might expect, perhaps because young children are innately prepared to notice only particular kinds of syntactic regularities present in the speech of adults.

A person who knows how to speak English, therefore, has acquired a great deal of tacit knowledge about the linguistic conventions of English-speaking people—about how to pronounce the language, about how things are named in the language, about how to form different types of grammatical

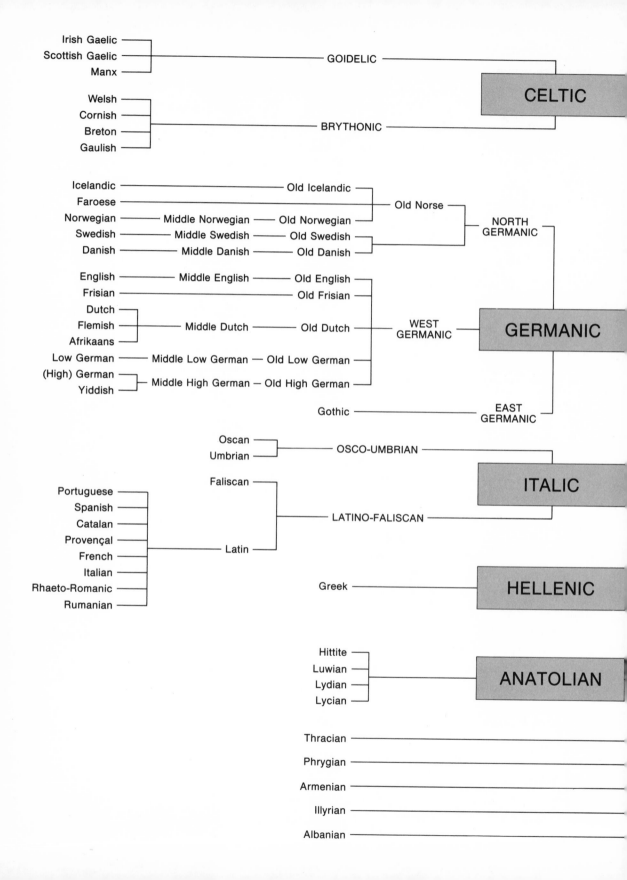

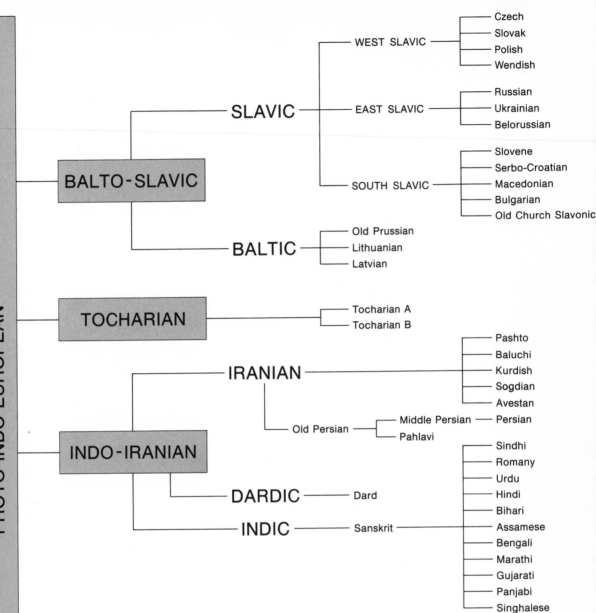

PROTO-INDO-EUROPEAN

BALTO-SLAVIC

SLAVIC

WEST SLAVIC
- Czech
- Slovak
- Polish
- Wendish

EAST SLAVIC
- Russian
- Ukrainian
- Belorussian

SOUTH SLAVIC
- Slovene
- Serbo-Croatian
- Macedonian
- Bulgarian
- Old Church Slavonic

BALTIC
- Old Prussian
- Lithuanian
- Latvian

TOCHARIAN
- Tocharian A
- Tocharian B

INDO-IRANIAN

IRANIAN
- Pashto
- Baluchi
- Kurdish
- Sogdian
- Avestan

Old Persian
- Middle Persian — Persian
- Pahlavi

DARDIC — Dard

INDIC — Sanskrit
- Sindhi
- Romany
- Urdu
- Hindi
- Bihari
- Assamese
- Bengali
- Marathi
- Gujarati
- Panjabi
- Singhalese

In 1786 Sir William Jones pointed out the strong relation among Sanskrit, Greek and Latin: "no philologer could examine them all three, without believing them to have sprung from some common source, which, perhaps, no longer exists." In 1816 Franz Bopp confirmed Jones's observation and founded the new science of comparative grammar. In 1822 Jacob Grimm announced his law for systematic sound shifts from Greek, Latin and Sanskrit into the Germanic languages, and in 1875 Karl Verner accounted for the apparent exceptions to Grimm's law. From such studies it has been possible to establish the historical relations among extinct and living languages and to reconstruct the salient features of proto-Indo-European, a language that is assumed to have been the common antecedent spoken more than 6,000 years ago, possibly in eastern Europe. The chart shows the developmental relations among the principal languages of the Indo-European family. A parallel chart (overleaf) indicates the developmental relations among the principal languages of the Indo-Chinese family.

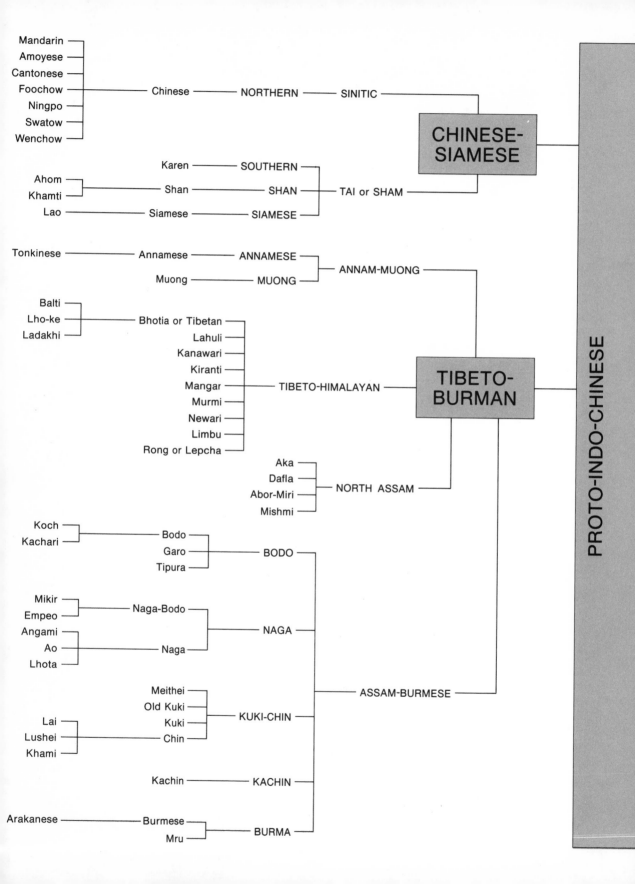

sentences. For all practical purposes, however, this knowledge of linguistic conventions can remain implicit, at the level of simply knowing how.

In school our teachers try to make us self-conscious about what we know how to do: they try to turn knowing how into knowing that. Unfortunately, many schoolteachers emphasize prescriptive rules of good usage and neglect the descriptive rules that are fundamental to any scientific understanding of language. Perhaps justifiably, the teacher is concerned that pupils learn "how to do it correctly." A scientist is less concerned with good usage—whatever you do is correct if everybody you talk to also does it—than with how people are able to use language at all.

Speech, the outward manifestation of the underlying system of knowledge that we call language, is a uniquely human activity. Other animals have other ways to communicate. We can sharpen our conception of human language by considering animal communication and by reviewing what little is known about how language might have evolved. With this perspective, we will next consider our ability to produce and to perceive speech at the rapid rates of conversational interaction.

In order to understand why speech is what it is, however, we must also consider what language is. A look at the syntactic and lexical components of language will make explicit some of the knowledge that normally remains implicit and will demonstrate how complicated human language really is.

Because babies are not born knowing a language or even knowing what a language is, we will also have to consider how they can master it so rapidly and how they come to accept linguistic conventions when no one can explain to them what the conventions are. Much of their learning must depend on insight into the contexts in which language is used. I will close with a discussion of conversational interactions and of the kind of problem solving that is involved in reconstructing a speaker's meaning from the hints he provides by the words he utters.

Each of these topics has been explored in great detail. In order to present a coherent account, I have selected in each case the lines of research that seem to me to bear most directly on the shared concern to understand the underlying nature of our human capacity for language.

The ancients assumed our incredible gift for language meant we are endowed by the gods with immortal souls. Perhaps we are, but modern science does not accept miracles as serious explanations. Today we demand a naturalistic account, and little by little, such an account is emerging. The account dispels some of the mystery, but it only heightens our respect for the complexity of language and for the mental powers of an organism capable of mastering and using it.

2

Animal Communication

Scientific statements should be objective—it should be possible to test whether they are true or false. Knowing a language is a personal thing. How can we make objective, testable statements about something that is normally so private and unselfconscious? How can we step outside our everyday use of language and see it as an object for scientific investigation? Clearly, we must adopt an impersonal attitude toward it. How do we do that?

One way is to look at human language as a particular form of communication, one among many alternative varieties. If we can see it side by side with other forms of communication, we will have taken a first step toward putting it in scientific perspective.

Scientists who believe there are other civilizations somewhere out in space have argued that we should try to communicate with them. Because humankind is only a few millenniums out of the Stone Age, chances are good that any extraterrestrial civilization we could reach would be far more advanced; its members could teach us a great deal. This argument assumes, of course, that they would be interested in communicating with us. They might view us and our civilization much as we view the social insects. There is no evidence that insects have learned anything by coming in contact with us. On the other hand, insects are not very good at learning, but we are.

When we look around our own planet, we find a variety of species that have evolved different ways of communicating. Ants, for example, communicate chemically by laying down trails for other ants to follow. Bees communicate about the location of food by performing elaborate dances and producing sounds when they return to the hive. Whales can communicate over great distances through the water by emitting complex tones. Other species of animals have their own species-specific forms of signaling.

We have learned much about communication by studying animals. We have learned, for example, that not all animals that communicate learn to communicate; insects, for example, communicate instinctively. If intelligent beings from outer space were to take the same interest in us that we have taken in other species, they would discover that we have a capacity to learn. They might try to teach us something, if only to test the limits of our ability.

Such speculation is more than idle talk not only because it could happen some day but because it gives us a mirror in which to view ourselves as we explore the abilities of simpler organisms. Experiments that teach apes to communicate with us by hand gestures, for example, give us a glimpse of the difficulties inherent in communication between intelligent beings at different levels of evolutionary development. Our friends from outer space—if, indeed, they are friends—will not find it easy to help us. They will have to be very patient.

It is difficult for us to communicate with other animals because we are different from them. Apes, for example, do not share our talent for vocal imitation. Some kinds of birds—parrots and myna birds—have an ability to mimic sounds but lack the intelligence to originate interesting messages. The dolphin, which seems to share with man both intelligence and a capacity for vocal imitation, lives in a world so different from ours that it has been difficult for us to break its code.

Looking at human speech as but one of many different species-specific forms of communication is like looking at humankind through the wrong end of a telescope. In spite of the difficulties, however, studies of animal communication offer an antidote for our usual preoccupation with human language. The perspective can be illustrated with two well-analyzed examples: birds and apes.

The first step in studying how animals use sounds for communication is to record their sounds under natural conditions. Then, by listening to these recordings and analyzing their acoustic properties, we can try to sort them into categories and to estimate the size of the species' acoustic vocabulary. It turns out that categorization is not always possible. Some species do use discrete, distinguishable categories of sounds, but other species seem to use a gradation of sounds—more intense sounds for more intense emotions, for example—with no obvious category boundaries. Where categorization is possible, however, the largest vocabularies are found for birds and mammals; invertebrates, fishes, amphibians and reptiles are far less versatile. Moreover, if we exclude human beings, birds and mammals are not very different in the size of their vocabularies; different species of birds may use between five and about 15 different categories of sound, whereas the range for monkeys and apes is from five to about 20 or 30.

In most birds, it is easy to distinguish between a variety of short calls and the song, which is usually produced only by males. From observation of the circumstances under which the short calls are used, they can be assigned various functions: a flight call, a social call, an alarm call, a courtship call. The song, on the other hand, is heard only at certain times of year. As the breeding season approaches and his level of sex hormones rises, the male will begin to vocalize the song characteristic of his species, sometimes in response to social stimulation but often spontaneously. The song is the loudest vocalization in his vocabulary, and during the reproductive season, it is the one most often heard. The song not only serves to attract a mate, it also broadcasts continuously the male's location and establishes his territorial rights.

The alarm calls of various woodland birds are often similar, but their songs are not. Survival of the species depends not only on the avoidance of predators, for which all birds have similar needs, but also on successful reproduction, for which each bird must be able to recognize members of its own species. Because the song of each species must be species-specific, new species of birds could not evolve unless birds were capable of relatively rapid evolutionary changes in their vocalizations.

Perhaps it is this need for the rapid establishment of distinctive songs that created a role for vocal learning in some birds. There is no evidence that learning plays an important part in the development of calls, but it can be very important in the development of the male song. For example, if a male white-crowned sparrow is raised in social isolation, without an opportunity to hear other sparrows, he develops an abnormal song. The period between 10 and 50 days of age seems to be critical for this learning, because after that time no amount of exposure to the normal song will enable the previously isolated bird to learn it. Moreover, exposure to the song of another species does not cause the isolated bird to learn an alien song. Merely hearing a song is not enough; the bird must hear the song of his own species—which indicates that his ability to hear particular patterns of sound must have evolved along with his ability to vocalize them and illustrates how experience and hereditary predispositions can interact in normal development.

There is usually a delay of several months between the time a young white-crowned sparrow hears the song of his own species and the time he is ready to sing it. If the bird is deafened during this period, after he has heard the song but before he is ready to sing it, he will not produce a normal song. Presumably, the early experience of hearing the song lays down a pattern, but if the bird cannot hear his own song, he cannot tell whether he is following that pattern or not. On the other hand, if an adult bird is deafened after he has mastered the song, deafness has no effect on his singing.

Some scientists see a similarity between these results, which establish that there is a critical period for song learning, and certain observations of how children learn to speak. Up to about the age of 10 or 12 years, children can learn to produce the exact speech sounds they hear around them, including even subtle details of accent and dialect that no one deliberately teaches them. Beyond that age such learning becomes difficult; few adults can learn to speak a foreign language without an accent that is detectable by a native speaker. Moreover, children who are born deaf acquire in-

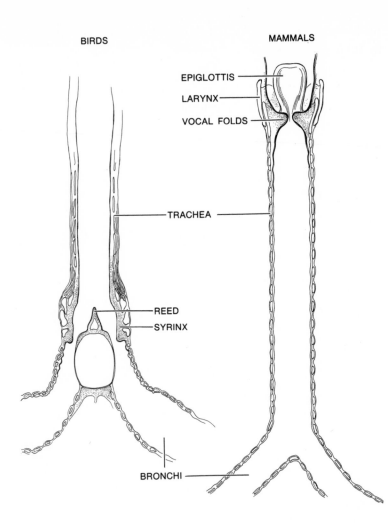

BIRDS

MAMMALS

EPIGLOTTIS

LARYNX

VOCAL FOLDS

TRACHEA

REED

SYRINX

BRONCHI

Voice in birds is produced by the syrinx, a modification of the lower end of the trachea. Voice in mammals is produced by the larynx, a modification of upper end of trachea.

telligible speech only with great difficulty and never with completely natural pronunciation and intonation.

The consequences of deafness or of missing the critical period for learning exact sound patterns are less drastic for people than for birds, because people can be taught a serviceable approximation of the correct sounds, whereas birds, as far as we know, cannot. Still, the parallel suggests that children, like birds, are born with an innate predisposition to develop certain kinds of vocal communication and not others. In this connection, it is interesting that if a bird is allowed to hear recordings of the song during the critical period between 10 and 50 days of age, song learning can occur in total social isolation. Apparently the vocalization is intrinsically rewarding in itself, because learning the song does not depend on the occurrence of any extrinsic reward as a consequence of producing it.

One curious resemblance to the human condition is that some birds, like human beings but unlike all other animals that have been studied, are bilaterally asymmetrical with respect to the neural control of vocalization. If, for example, we take an adult male chaffinch in full song and cut the nerves on the right side, going from the brain to the syrinx, only minor changes in the song will result, but if we cut the nerves on the left side, the song will disintegrate and cannot be relearned. On the other hand, if we take a young male chaffinch that has not yet come into full song and cut the nerves on the left side, he will develop a normal song. Normal development can occur as long as either side is intact. In the young bird, either side of the brain is capable of learning the song, but once the learning has occurred, it is localized on one side of the brain and cannot be relearned on the other.

Such similarities should not blind us to the obvious differences between bird songs and human speech. Trying to teach a sparrow to speak English would certainly fail, although the bird can learn particular patterns of vocalization. However, some students of animal behavior have felt that such an attempt might not fail with the great apes. Because communication with other animals has been a human fantasy at least since Aesop, these experiments have attracted wide interest. How fascinating it would be to hear a chimpanzee explain what it is like to be a chimpanzee!

About two dozen calls have been distinguished in the vocalizations of wild chimpanzees, but little is known about the functions of their various hoots, calls and grunts. Most scientists assume they express emotions and are an automatic part of the animals' instinctive responses to pleasant or fearful situations. More study may reveal differentiations that have been overlooked, but at present it appears that sound is merely one aspect—and not a particularly important aspect—of chimpanzee communication. There is no question that chimpanzees communicate, because they maintain an elaborate social organization, but seeing, touching and smelling are as important to them as hearing. Nothing resembling a preliminary form of protospeech has been reported in field studies of wild chimpanzees.

This fact may puzzle anyone accustomed to associating intelligence with facility in using language, for these animals are undoubtedly intelligent. They are even able to manufacture and use tools (for example, sticks for fishing termites out of their nests), an ability that was once considered solely the prerogative of human beings. Chimpanzees probably have patterns of learned behavior that, like human culture, are passed on from one generation to the next. In the laboratory they have demonstrated their ability to learn distinctions and solve problems, sometimes with surprising ingenuity. If they are so smart, why don't they talk?

This question leads naturally to the next: If they are so smart, could they be taught to talk? The answer, apparently, is a flat no. About 30 years ago in Florida, two psychologists, Keith and Catherine Hayes, adopted a female chimpanzee, named her Viki and raised her as if she were their own child, making every effort to teach her to speak English. After five years of training, using all available techniques of teaching and speech therapy, Viki was able to utter three words that sounded approximately like "mama," "papa" and "cup." The chimp used "cup" to ask for a drink of water, but "mama" and "papa" were used to refer to anything else she wanted, not to her foster parents. And even these three utterances were produced with difficulty. In other respects, Viki was surprisingly intelligent. On various tests requiring conceptual distinctions, Viki scored as well as average children her own age, in spite of the fact that she had no words to represent the concepts involved. On one test that required a discrimination between pictures of people and pictures of animals, Viki responded correctly— but she put her own picture in the group with people.

Viki's failure was so convincing that it was 20 years before anyone tried again to communicate with a chimpanzee, and then the approach was entirely different. This time the question was, If they are so smart, could they be taught to communicate with us? Instead of spoken language, the gestural language of the deaf was used. Because chimpanzees in the wild are responsive to gestures but have little voluntary control over their vocalizations, why not try to teach them to use the American Sign Language (ASL)? R. Allen and Beatrice T. Gardner, psychologists in Reno, Nevada, adopted a female chimpanzee, named her Washoe and communicated with her by signs they learned from a dictionary of ASL. Compared with Viki, Washoe made spectacular progress. By the age of four, Washoe had learned to

AMERICAN SIGN LANGUAGE   DANISH SIGN LANGUAGE   CHINESE SIGN LANGUAGE

Is Sign Language Pictorial?

The gestures that make up the vocabularies of the sign languages of the deaf probably originated in pantomime of the sort that two hearing people who speak different languages might use spontaneously. With repeated use the gestures became standardized and abbreviated into conventional signs, but many of them have retained an iconic, or pictorial, quality. When people who do not know sign language are shown one of these iconic signs and told its meaning, they usually agree about the relation between sign and meaning. The pictorial relation does not determine what the sign must be, however. The drawings above show the sign for "tree" in the American, Danish and Chinese sign languages. All three signs are pictorial, but all are different. When people who do not know sign language are shown one of these signs and asked to guess its meaning, they usually fail to do so.

respond appropriately to about 500 signs and could reliably make more than 80 signs. Most important, she generalized these signs to objects other than the ones used in training and even to absent objects. For example, the sign for "dog" was originally learned from a picture of a dog but was generalized to other pictures and to real dogs; signs for "dog" and "listen dog" came to be used when she heard a dog barking in the distance. The sign for "open" was learned in connection with a particular door but was generalized to other doors, then to any closed containers, like jars, boxes, drawers and eventually to a water faucet.

The Gardners avoided formal teaching of the structure of ASL—its rules of combination, for example—in order to observe spontaneous developments. Of course, the human signers tried to model good ASL. These conditions are similar to those under which human children develop the structural features of their native language. Washoe's first combination ("gimme sweet") occurred at the age of 20 months; by the time she was 34 months old, the Gardners had recorded 330 combinations. This rate of development is considerably slower than it is for children, but the fact that combinations occurred at all indicates that chimpanzees are even more intelligent than had been suspected.

With this encouragement, the next step was to ask whether a chimp could be trained to differentiate between the same signs in different orders. In California, David and Ann Premack undertook to train a female chimp named Sarah. Instead of gestures from ASL, however, Sarah was taught to use plastic tokens varying in size, shape and color. She was taught to associate different things with each token: one token stood for Sarah herself, one for the experimenter, one for bananas, one for chocolate, one for pails and so on, and other tokens stood for relations or actions. The tokens bore no resemblance to the things they signified.

From a practical point of view, plastic tokens are inferior to gestures—without her tokens, Sarah could not communicate—but from the point of view of an experimenter interested in sequential order, they had an obvious advantage. It is much easier to see the order of a sequence of tokens than it is to remember the order of a sequence of gestures. Sarah

Sarah, a female chimpanzee, was trained to communicate by placing plastic tokens in sequence. She arranged tokens for "Mary give chocolate Sarah" on a magnetic board. Mary was the experimenter; the vertical order was Sarah's own idea.

spontaneously used a vertical order, and the experimenters adapted to her preference.

In some of the simplest experiments, Sarah was taught to use tokens that meant "same" and "different." First, a token that was used as a sign for "?" was placed between two other tokens. If the two tokens were the same, Sarah learned to replace the token "?" with the token for "same"; if they were different, she learned to replace "?" with "different." Once she learned this, she was given sequences of tokens corresponding to "? same apple," for example; Sarah removed the token for "?" and replaced it with the token for "apple." Then she learned tokens for "yes" and "no," which she could use appropriately to replace "?" in sequences like "? apple same banana."

Sarah learned token-names for colors. After she had learned a few of them, she was given the token-sentence "Brown color-of chocolate." Then, when given the sentence "Sarah take brown," she selected the brown disk from an array of differently colored disks. Because no actual chocolate was seen when brown was defined, Sarah must have thought of chocolate and remembered its color—which would seem to settle the claim that chimps cannot use signs for absent objects.

In some of the most complicated experiments, Sarah was given complex token-sequences of the form "Red on green if-then Sarah take apple; green on red if-then Sarah take banana," in which case, if a red card was on top of a green card, Sarah took the apple and not the banana that was available—which would seem to settle the claim that chimps are insensitive to the order in a sequence of signs.

Since Washoe and Sarah blazed the trail, language experiments with chimpanzees and other great apes have sprung up overnight like mushrooms. What does it all mean? Enthusiasts claim that it means apes really are capable of using and understanding human language, although they will never be able to speak; even skeptics are forced to admit that apes must be capable of much more abstract, conceptual thought than they had suspected. Critics, on the other hand, claim that this preoccupation with teaching apes a human language has distorted scientific study of the natural communication systems of nonhuman primates.

These studies raise as many questions as they answer, which, at some stages of a science, can be a good thing. With respect to human language, the questions they raise can be put this way. Under appropriate conditions, apes can learn the rudiments of communication techniques that bear certain formal resemblances to human language, yet there is no evidence from field studies that these intelligent animals make any natural use of these latent abilities. Apparently, apes get along in the wild perfectly well without this kind of communication. So the questions are, Why were our ancestors different? What conditions could have existed to favor the survival of those early hominids who were best able to communicate linguistically?

3

The Evolution of Human Language

Although Charles Darwin's *Origin of Species* in 1859 made the case for evolutionary theory and implied the organic evolution of man, it left three critical questions unanswered. One of these, concerning the mechanism of hereditary transmission, has now been answered definitively. The remaining two questions concern the origin of life and the origin of human language, events that occurred so long ago that we will never have definitive answers. With respect to the origin of life, however, we now have some chemically plausible hypotheses. The third question—What is the origin of human language?—has never received a satisfactory answer.

It is not that we have been unable to devise hypotheses to replace the biblical story that language began when Adam gave names to everything. Just the opposite. We have many hypotheses but no obvious way to choose among them.

Speculation about the origins of human language is as old as history. Attempts to formulate plausible scientific hypotheses can be traced back to the 17th century, and each proposal aroused new storms of debate. The controversy became so heated during the 19th century that in 1866 the Linguistic Society of Paris prohibited further discussion of it. Although the ban had little effect, the question did eventually fall into disfavor; for many years serious linguists dismissed it as unanswerable. Recently, there has been a renewal of interest.

Although there is disagreement about the exact time, language as we know it today probably appeared relatively late in the unrecorded prehistory of humans. Moreover, it probably happened only once. That is to say, all languages are probably derived from a single source, a language probably spoken originally in East Africa.

What has stirred the imaginations of those inclined to speculate has been the possible sequence of events leading up to the appearance of modern language. Did our ancestors jump suddenly from an apelike form of communication to human language? Did the capacity for language result from some single genetic mutation? Or was there a sequence of organic adaptations and communicative innovations leading only gradually to modern language? If the process was gradual or if a number of sudden mutations contributed to it, what sequence of social and environmental events could have shaped it? If there were prelinguistic forms of communication more complex than animal cries, what were they like?

Such questions have stimulated a wealth of ingenious guesses. Before any hypothesis can gain general acceptance, however, it will have to be consistent with an enormous range of heterogeneous facts. The evolution of our capacity for language cannot be explained without taking into account all aspects of the evolution of modern man. But the kind of evidence that might settle these issues is simply unobtainable. As long as the specific outlines of human evolution are themselves speculative and controversial, hypotheses about the nature and adaptive advantages of prelinguistic forms of communication will remain impossible to evaluate. This difficulty, however, has not inhibited speculation—which is all right as long as we recognize it as speculation, not fact.

One early hypothesis was that modern language developed from a gestural system. Strong versions held that it was totally gestural at first; weak versions, that gestural and vocal signals supplemented each other. The discovery that apes can learn to communicate by gestures has revived interest in gestural theories of the origin of language, even though none of the living apes is in the ancestral line of *Homo sapiens*. One imagines various scenarios in which the earliest man-apes, once they stood erect and their hands

Interpretation of the Fossil Hominid Record

Below is a cladogram—a branching diagram based on shared characteristics—that represents a provisional theory of the relations among fossil hominids. This cladogram is an attempt to summarize the basic data presently available in the fossil hominid record. It is impossible to decide whether Neanderthal man is more similar to *Homo erectus* (node A) or to *Homo sapiens sapiens* (node B), and the cladogram reflects this ambiguity.

Opposite are two of several phylogenetic trees that would be compatible with the evidence summarized in the cladogram. A phylogenetic tree incorporates information about the time at which the fossils lived and represents hypotheses about their evolutionary relationships: whether they are related as direct descendants by linear evolution or as "sis-

ters" by splitting into two distinct species that lived at the same time (speciation). Thus, a tree is more speculative than a cladogram and is further removed from the basic data. (Broken wide bars indicate that fossils are only tentatively assigned to a species; broken narrow bars represent inferential lines of descent, which are not based on fossil evidence.)

A scenario attempts to relate a phylogenetic tree to information about ecology and adaptation; a particular tree can be used as the basis for a variety of scenarios, which are yet further removed from the basic data. Because scenarios introduce hypotheses that are usually impossible to test empirically, they must be judged on grounds of plausibility rather than truth. Hence, the usual degree of controversy that characterizes this field of science.

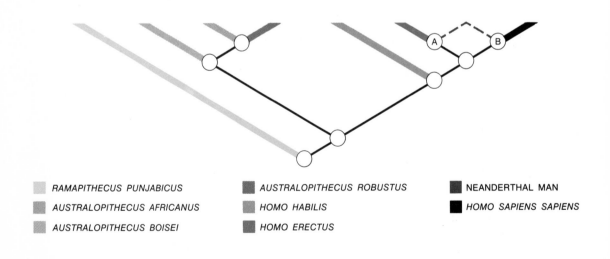

RAMAPITHECUS PUNJABICUS

AUSTRALOPITHECUS AFRICANUS

AUSTRALOPITHECUS BOISEI

AUSTRALOPITHECUS ROBUSTUS

HOMO HABILIS

HOMO ERECTUS

NEANDERTHAL MAN

HOMO SAPIENS SAPIENS

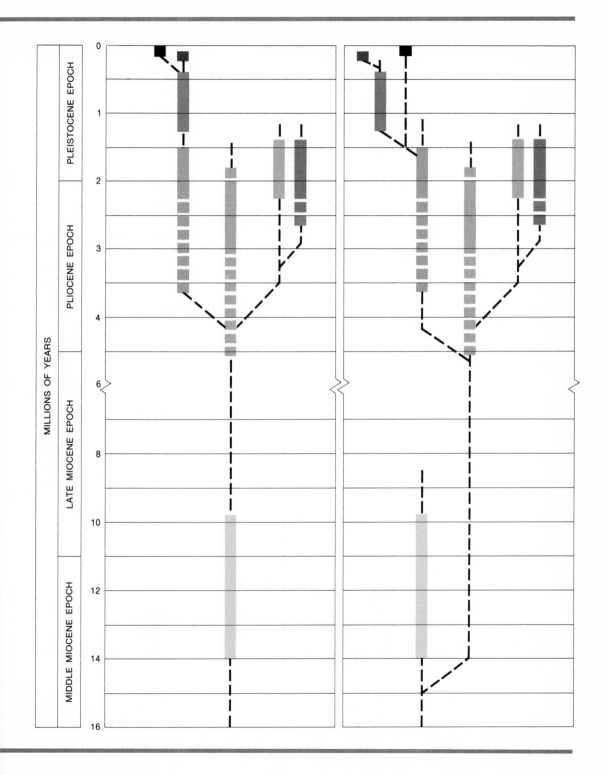

were freed, organized complex social interactions by hand signals.

The problem for a gestural theory is explaining how, why and when gestures gave way to vocal communication. It has been proposed, for example, that when hand signals were impractical, the hand gesture was imitated by tongue movements accompanied by vocalization. In the absence of data, theorists can be remarkably imaginative.

A vocal theorist, on the other hand, might argue that man evolved from apes who happened to have a relatively large vocabulary of discrete or graded calls, which were initially used instinctively and automatically. Then, through a series of evolutionary steps, these calls were brought under voluntary control. For example, an alarm call that was initially broadcast to everyone by any alarmed animal might come to be directed only to those animals that were judged to be unaware of the danger.

Vocal theorists have suggested that an instinctual core of vocal signals shared by all hominids might explain why all the spoken languages of the world are still so much alike. Before any recognizable precursor to human language could evolve, however, our ancestors had to become capable of combining vocal signals in sequences having indefinitely many different meanings. One view of how this capacity for combinatorial elaboration appeared holds that there was some important genetic mutation, probably about 100,000 years ago, that suddenly made human language possible. Thereafter, our ancestors, who had shared millions of years of common evolutionary change, rapidly dispersed over the earth, racial differentiation began and geographic isolation fostered the development of many different, mutually unintelligible languages.

An alternative view is that the combinatorial productivity of language resulted not from some genetic specialization for language but from a gradual increase in general intelligence that accompanied the evolutionary increase in the size of the brain. According to this view, language emerged when intelligence reached some critical level adequate to support it, much as water turns suddenly to ice when the temperature is gradually lowered until the freezing point is

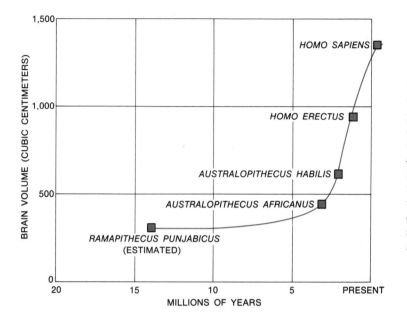

BRAIN VOLUME (CUBIC CENTIMETERS)

1,500

1,000

500

0

HOMO SAPIENS

HOMO ERECTUS

AUSTRALOPITHECUS HABILIS

AUSTRALOPITHECUS AFRICANUS

RAMAPITHECUS PUNJABICUS
(ESTIMATED)

20   15   10   5   PRESENT

MILLIONS OF YEARS

The brain size of our ancestors began increasing rapidly about five million years ago. On the evolutionary scale, an increase from 400 to 1,400 cubic centimeters in five million years is a spectacular rate of change. During that time, however, man went through about 250,000 generations, which is an increase of only 0.004 cubic centimeter per generation; the increase in size may be remarkable, but it is certainly not impossible.

reached. Hominids went on becoming more and more intelligent until, relatively late in the evolution of *Homo sapiens*, somebody was intelligent enough to think of inventing language, at which point organic evolution ceased and cultural evolution began. This view is no longer as popular as it once was.

The assumption that an increase in general intelligence confers some enormous selective advantage on the intelligent species leaves one wondering why no other species took this evolutionary route. The further assumption that language was an invention—that increased general intelligence suffices to explain the human capacity for language—does not stand up to the available evidence. For example, we have learned that chimpanzees (with brains of about 400 cubic centimeters) are intelligent enough to have rudimentary language, yet they do not. Even more important, the fossil record tells us that cultural evolution, in the form of toolmaking and food sharing, was under way 2,000,000 years ago, long before human organic evolution achieved its current state. Cultural evolution must have influenced organic evolution. According to this view, our human brains do not merely enable us to acquire culture, culture is itself an

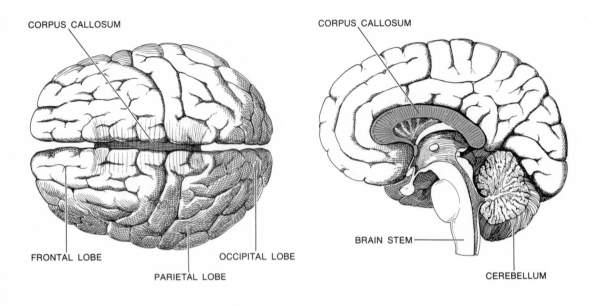

CORPUS CALLOSUM

FRONTAL LOBE

OCCIPITAL LOBE

PARIETAL LOBE

CORPUS CALLOSUM

BRAIN STEM

CEREBELLUM

Split Brains, Split Minds

The brain consists of two hemispheres: the left hemisphere controls the right side of the body, and the right controls the left side. In the normal human brain these two hemispheres are connected by discrete bundles of nerve fibers, called commissures, by which neural activity in one cerebral hemisphere is duplicated in the other. The largest of these is the great cerebral commissure, or corpus callosum (a fiber tract containing more than 200,000,000 neurons).

Brain surgeons, in an effort to stop the spread of epileptic seizures from one hemisphere to the other, have cut the connecting tract in some patients. Studies of such patients have led to an understanding of the functions of the corpus callosum. A person's general behavior seems to be little affected by the operation, but careful psychological testing reveals that the patient's mental life is split when the brain is split. One hemisphere is not aware of information presented only to the other hemisphere. Consequently, binocular depth perception is impaired, coordination of movements of the two hands together is disturbed and manipulospatial abilities of the right hand are limited.

The most striking demonstration of the split mind, however, is that the person in whom the corpus callosum has been severed is unable to report verbally on information presented exclusively to the right hemisphere. Speech is controlled (in the great majority of people) by the left hemisphere. If a picture is shown briefly in the left visual field, which projects exclusively to the right hemisphere, the person will say "I didn't see anything," because the visual information is not available to the hemisphere that controls speech. The right hemisphere's awareness of the picture can nevertheless be demonstrated by correct tactual identification of the pictured object with the left hand.

ingredient of our organically based capacities. The human brain cannot function normally without it.

From all we know about evolution, it is difficult to doubt that there must have been some form of vocal communication (perhaps supplemented by gestures) intermediate between primitive grunts and hoots and the languages of modern man, although no living species exists to give us a hint of what it might have been. Increased brain size was one factor that we know was operating, but it may not have been the most important. Changes in the organization of the brain, in the vocal tract and in the auditory system may have been more important.

In modern man, speech is nearly always controlled by the left hemisphere of the brain. In most normal people, any information that comes into the right hemisphere (from the left hand, say, or the left half of the visual field) must be transferred, via the corpus callosum, to the left hemisphere before it can be talked about. If the two hemispheres are surgically disconnected, a person can talk only about information that is available to the left hemisphere. Moreover, within the left hemisphere important speech and language functions are localized in Broca's and Wernicke's areas; we know that damage to these areas can seriously interfere with the ability to produce or understand speech. The fact that these functions, which are uniquely human, are lateralized in the left hemisphere, taken together with the fact that there is no comparable lateralization of vocal functions in the brains of other living primates, is sometimes taken to mean that neural centers specific to speech must have evolved in the left hemisphere and not in the right hemisphere. There is nothing genetically fixed about the left hemisphere that makes it uniquely suited to control speech and language, however, because the right hemisphere can take over these functions if the left is injured early in life. What seems to have evolved is not a special structure in the left hemisphere but rather a more general disposition to acquire linguistic communication, plus a capacity for this acquisition to become lateralized—usually, but not necessarily, in the left hemisphere.

Neural mechanisms controlling the motor movements

required for articulate speech also seem to be specialized. Human beings have a special link between the auditory system and the speech-production system, presumably because successful communication depends not on muscular movements as such but rather on their acoustic consequences. Most motor performances are guided predominantly by feedback from the muscles and joints, but in the case of speech muscles, auditory feedback is more important. So important, in fact, that when it is missing, as it is in congenitally deaf children, learning to produce intelligible speech is very difficult.

The neurological adaptations to language that are implied by lateralization and auditory control probably did not result from any single mutation. Moreover, to produce the full range of sounds used in modern languages, the vocal tract must have a throat cavity as well as a mouth cavity, which means that the larynx must descend into the neck in order to create a larger throat cavity than is found in living apes. And the auditory system must evolve a speech-specific

Speech and language functions are localized in Broca's and Wernicke's areas in the left hemisphere of the human brain. Broca's area plays a role in the production of speech, translating information from other speech areas of the brain into actual speech. Wernicke's area is involved in the comprehension of the auditory input and the monitoring of speech output. Damage to these regions can seriously interfere with the ability either to produce or understand speech.

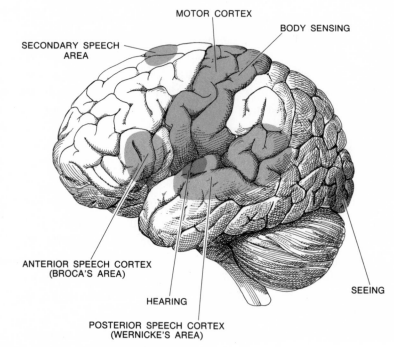

MOTOR CORTEX

BODY SENSING

SECONDARY SPEECH
AREA

ANTERIOR SPEECH CORTEX
(BROCA'S AREA)

HEARING

POSTERIOR SPEECH CORTEX
(WERNICKE'S AREA)

SEEING

system capable of recognizing that speech is different from other sounds and able to analyze the distinctive features of spoken sounds at rapid rates. These specializations did not evolve overnight, either.

In short, human language requires so many special and anatomically unrelated adaptations that it seems unlikely they all appeared simultaneously, in a single mutation. It is reasonable to assume, therefore, that vocal communication evolved—that there must have been intermediate forms of vocal communication—even though how it happened is anybody's guess.

None of the physiological or anatomical adaptations basic to the capacity for human language is unique to man. What seems to have been unique to man is that all these adaptations—including a predisposition to communicate, an ability to mimic sound, the intelligence to learn and to label and relate classes of objects and events, and a sensitivity to differences in the sequences of signs—came together in a single organism at a time when long-term variations in temperature (the glacial-interglacial cycles) created sufficient ecological stress to favor social cooperation and promote natural selection. This convergence was an enormously improbable evolutionary accident.

If there were prelinguistic forms of vocal communication, none of the hominids that used them have survived; there is today an enormous gap in communicative abilities between human beings and all other animals. The 19th-century assumption that people not advanced in technology must be biologically inferior and therefore must speak inferior, perhaps infrahuman languages has been totally discredited. On the basis of all that is known about the languages of the world, linguists maintain that there are today no primitive languages. The phonology, morphology and syntax of exotic languages have proved to be every bit as rich and complex as (often more complex than) those of any Indo-European language.

It is well known, of course, that languages change over time. Today, for example, English-speaking students must take special courses in order to learn Old English. An enormous amount of research has gone into establishing the chronology of developments within the Indo-European family of languages. However, most linguists carefully refrain from attributing to those changes the kind of "progress" that, during the 19th century, was supposed to characterize evolutionary change.

It is necessary, therefore, to respect the dignity of exotic languages spoken in the so-called underdeveloped parts of the world. Nevertheless, there are clear differences to be seen in the vocabularies of those languages, differences closely associated with the development of modern society and technology. The languages of industrially developed nations have many words for which there are no equivalents in exotic languages, words for concepts, relations and institutions that can only be translated by elaborate descriptive phrases. Indeed, these lexical deficiencies pose a major cultural barrier for any underdeveloped country that wants to move rapidly into the 20th century.

Perhaps the best-documented instance of lexical evolution, one that illustrates the difference between organic and cultural change, is the evolution of color terminology.

Color perception in primates is organized around three opponent processes. Neurophysiological and psychological research has shown that black/white, red/green and yellow/blue perception is mediated by independent neural systems. In English color terminology, the opposition of these neural systems is reflected in the fact that although we have color mixtures that we call gray, purple or blue-green there are no such color names as whitish-black, greenish-red or blue-yellow.

Black, white, red, green, yellow and blue are psychological primaries, and in English we have different names for all six of them. Many languages, however, do not have distinct names for all six primary colors. People who speak these languages are not organically inferior; they are not color-blind. When necessary, they can identify colors for which they have no basic term by using descriptive phrases or by using the names of familiar objects having that color. The deficiency is not in their vision but in their lexicon. Apparently, color is not sufficiently important in their culture for such a naming convention to develop.

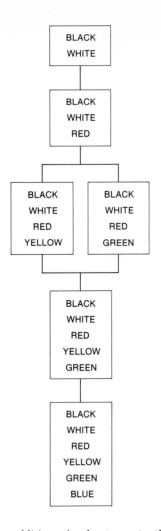

BLACK
WHITE

BLACK
WHITE
RED

BLACK
WHITE
RED
YELLOW

BLACK
WHITE
RED
GREEN

BLACK
WHITE
RED
YELLOW
GREEN

BLACK
WHITE
RED
YELLOW
GREEN
BLUE

The addition of color terms to the vocabulary of a language follows an evolutionary sequence. When a language has just two color terms, they refer to black and white. If a third term is added, it refers to red; a fourth refers to yellow or green. A language with terms for five colors includes both yellow and green, and when a sixth color is named, it is blue.

Different languages have different numbers of basic color terms, and there is a pattern in the colors that are not named. Anthropologists have found that all languages have at least two basic color terms. If a language has only two color terms, they will divide the colors into what we might call light-warm (white, yellow, red) and dark-cool (black, blue, green). If a language has three basic color terms, they will refer to black, white and red. That is to say, if people who speak the language are shown a large color chart and asked to point to the best instances of colors to which these three terms refer, they will point to colors that are very close to what English speakers would choose as the best instances of black, white and red. Languages that have four basic color terms will also have a term for either yellow or green, but not both. If a language has five, it will have terms for both yellow and green. If it has six basic color terms, it will have a term for every one of the psychological primaries. If we assume that basic terms are never dropped from the vocabulary of a language, there would appear to be a fixed sequence of evolutionary stages through which all languages pass as their basic color vocabulary increases. That is to say, if the generalization applies to existing languages, it probably applied to past languages as well.

Obviously, lexical evolution is not organic evolution. No further organic evolution would be required for any living group to learn names for all the primary colors. Probably no further organic evolution would have been required for Cro-Magnon man to learn a modern language. But social evolution supplements the biological gift of language. The vocabulary of any language is a repository for all those categories and relations that previous generations deemed worthy of terminological recognition, a cultural heritage of common sense passed on from each generation to the next and slowly enriched from accumulated experience.

The linguist Morris Swadesh suggested that the rate of change of the core words in a lexicon is constant over time. From studies of Indo-European languages of known history at different times, using a list of 100 basic lexical concepts, he estimated the rate of change to be 14 percent per millennium. If this constant is assumed to apply generally, then

33

the percentage of cognate words (words derived historically from the same root) in two languages can be used to estimate how long ago they diverged from a common source language. In this model of language evolution it is assumed that cognate words can always be accurately recognized and that no words have been borrowed between languages. One reason for confining the comparisons to a basic list is that borrowing is less likely for words expressing the commonest ideas.

When Swadesh compared lists of words from languages spoken in distant parts of the world, his lexicostatistical technique yielded estimates in the neighborhood of 10 millenniums. In other words, if this method can be trusted, just 10,000 years ago everybody spoke the same language. Swadesh allowed, however, that lexical change may have been slower when social change and technological change were slower, and therefore, 10,000 years is probably an underestimation. But he thought that 100,000 years would probably be an overestimation.

Some caution must be indicated, however. Subsequent research has shown that the words used to express some meanings change more rapidly than the words used to express other meanings. Consequently, more-complicated statistical models have been devised, using rates of change that vary from about 8 to 50 percent per millennium for different parts of the list. However, even these more sophisticated models of lexical evolution do not give accurate predictions of the actual times at which different Indo-European languages are believed to have separated.

For example, the Germanic languages are believed to have divided into Scandinavian, English and German languages around 300 A.D., which was 1.7 millenniums ago. Lexical statistics consistently underestimate the time of separation. That is to say, there are more cognate words shared by these languages than there should be, which makes it necessary to assume that, in this case, the number of basic words borrowed back and forth between languages was not negligible. The assumption that languages evolve in isolation from one another is clearly too simple in a world where travel, conquests, commerce and literature create intimate contacts between them. Counting the number of cognate basic words shared by different languages can lead to a reasonably accurate reconstruction of the order in which languages separated, but estimates of the actual times at which these separations occurred are rough approximations at best.

If Swadesh's upper limit of 100,000 years is anywhere near correct, however, cultural evolution must have begun long before the appearance of human language as we know it today. Indisputably man-made stone tools more than 2,000,000 years old have been found in East Africa. Our human capacity for language must have been shaped by cultural as well as organic evolution.

Language and toolmaking are usually taken together as criteria of humanity. It is natural to think of them together—to think that the same intellectual and symbolic abilities required for language are also required to design and manufacture stone tools. Observations of chimpanzees, however, have shown that tool use and even rudimentary toolmaking occur spontaneously in the absence of language. Moreover, the technological progress in toolmaking achieved during the period from 1,500,000 to 500,000 years ago was negligible, suggesting a level of intellectual capacity well below that of modern man. It is difficult to imagine so little cultural innovation, so little dynamism, in organisms capable of human language. Conversely, it is easy to imagine that the increasingly rapid rate of technological development during the last 50,000 years has gone hand in hand with the evolution of language—that the ability to make tools and the ability to symbolize and communicate the toolmaking process have developed together. If this is the case, the evidence from technological evolution would seem to be consistent with Swadesh's estimates of the first emergence of human language as we know it today.

The true antiquity of human language could only be settled by tangible evidence, and that, of course, is lacking. There are no relics of language prior to the invention of writing. Most scholars assume that writing is no more than 5,000 years old, although engraved patterns found on batons and spear-throwers that are 30,000 years old suggest a much earlier use of complex notational systems, even though it is not known what the engravings represented. Writing had important cultural consequences of its own, and printing made possible the dissemination of written documents to large audiences. But these more recent developments need not be surveyed here.

In summary, although there has been much interesting speculation based on circumstantial evidence, we still do not know how the capacity for language evolved. Nor do we know why *Homo sapiens* developed a brain so much larger than was necessary for survival in the wild. It is difficult to believe that these two mysteries are unrelated, but what the relation really was we may never know.

4

The Source-Filter Theory

In 1971 the scientific world—or that part of it that happened to notice—was startled by the claim made by Philip Lieberman, then at the University of Connecticut, and Edmund Slocum Crelin, of Yale University, that Neanderthal man could not have produced the full range of human speech.

It was not the publication of another hypothesis about Neanderthals that was surprising. The large-brained, Stone Age hominid has been a mystery ever since the first discovery of his skull in 1856. His sudden appearance and disappearance in the fossil record and his relation to earlier and later European men pose questions that archaeologists and paleoanthropologists have never been able to settle.

The shock was that the new hypothesis concerned Neanderthal speech. Neanderthal skeletons are now well known, and the flint tools found with Neanderthal bones have been studied in detail. But bones and stones are durable objects, whereas few things are less durable than the sound of the human voice. What possible evidence about Neanderthal vocalizations could have survived since the last glacial period? The shock was not so much what was claimed as that serious scientists could find any basis for making such claims at all.

The evidence was in the bones, but interpreting it required an application of a new field of research: speech science. The historical origins of this field are in the middle of the 18th century, but its modern development began in

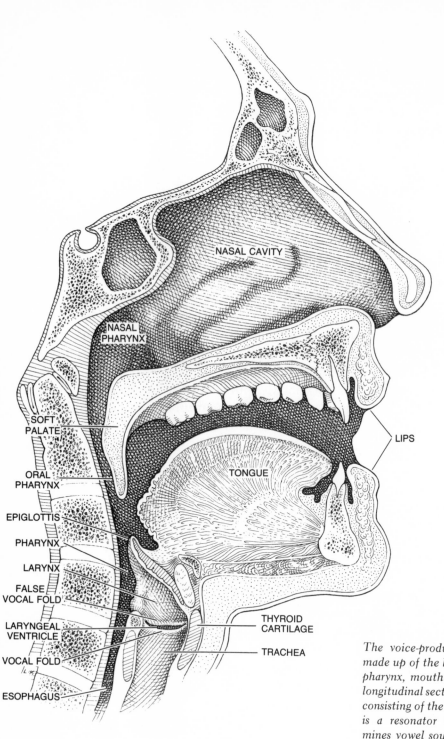

NASAL CAVITY

NASAL
PHARYNX

SOFT
PALATE

ORAL
PHARYNX

EPIGLOTTIS

PHARYNX

LARYNX

FALSE
VOCAL FOLD

LARYNGEAL
VENTRICLE

VOCAL FOLD

ESOPHAGUS

LIPS

TONGUE

THYROID
CARTILAGE

TRACHEA

The voice-producing mechanism is made up of the lungs and the larynx, pharynx, mouth and nose, shown in longitudinal section. The vocal tract, consisting of the pharynx and mouth, is a resonator whose shape determines vowel sounds. The shape can be modified by changes in position of the lips, jaw, tongue and larynx.

the 1930's and accelerated with the increasing availability of sophisticated electronic technology. The new speech science is a fascinating combination of muscular and neural physiology, physical acoustics and perceptual and cognitive psychology. Physiology is used to describe how the sounds of speech are produced, acoustics is used to analyze the sounds themselves and psychology is used to determine what aspects of those sounds are important for human communication. We must become familiar with this new science in order to see how it was possible to apply it to the speech abilities of extinct fossil hominids.

When we talk, air from our lungs is expelled in a controlled way through the larynx and the vocal tract—the throat (pharynx), mouth, teeth, lips and, for some sounds, the nose. Sound is produced by making constrictions in this system. The most important source of sound is in the larynx (the so-called voice box, or Adam's apple), where the vocal folds (infoldings of mucous membrane), or cords, can be brought together with just the right tension to vibrate—to release a rapid series of puffs of air into the vocal tract. How this laryngeal tone sounds, however, will depend on the shape of the vocal tract, which acts as a filter (a resonator that reinforces some frequencies of vibration and attenuates others). Not all speech sounds involve this laryngeal tone. Those that do are called voiced sounds. (Voiced and voiceless speech sounds will be discussed in chapter 5, "Speech.")

The source-filter theory of speech production was proposed in 1848 by the German physiologist Johannes Müller, and it is still the basic concept that guides research on the vocalizations of human beings and other animals. The vibration of the vocal folds is taken to be the source; the vocal tract is viewed as an acoustic tube that, depending on its shape and length, filters the source in different ways. The source-filter theory can be illustrated most easily for the vowel sounds, which are produced without the obstructions in the vocal tract that are characteristic of voiced consonants.

Consider the unstressed, neutral vowel schwa [ə], which forms the first syllable of the English word "about." Let us assume that a man has spoken this vowel and that the fundamental frequency of his voice was 100 hertz, or cycles per second (middle C on the piano is 262 hertz). The laryngeal tone, if it were unmodified by the vocal tract, would consist of this fundamental frequency plus harmonic overtones at 200 hertz, 300 hertz, 400 hertz and so on. Most of the sound energy would be in the fundamental, and the higher the frequency of the overtones, the less sound energy they would contain. This pattern is called the acoustic spectrum of the laryngeal tone. It would be much the same for any voiced sound produced with this fundamental frequency. If the laryngeal tone were produced at some other frequency—call it x hertz—the shape of the spectrum would be the same, but the overtones would occur at $2x$ hertz, $3x$ hertz, $4x$ hertz and so on.

From X-ray pictures of speakers producing this sound, it is possible to determine the exact shape of the vocal tract between the larynx and the lips. In the case of [ə], the tract can be approximated well enough by a uniform tube 17 centimeters long and open at one end. The lowest resonant frequency of such a tube can be calculated from its quarter wavelength. Because 17 centimeters is one quarter of the length of a sound wave that is 68 centimeters long, and because the velocity of sound in air at sea level is approximately 33,500 centimeters per second, the lowest resonant frequency will be 33,500/68, or about 500 hertz. Therefore, an overtone at 500 hertz will have just the right wavelength to be reinforced (to resonate) in this tube, and overtones below or above 500 hertz will be relatively weaker as a consequence of passing through it. At about 1,000 hertz a tube of this length will not resonate, and these frequencies will be attenuated, or partially filtered out. At 1,500 hertz, however, there is another resonant frequency, corresponding to the three-quarter wavelength, and at 2,500 hertz there is a third resonant frequency, corresponding to the five-quarter wavelength. Thus, the filtering produced by such a tube can be simply calculated; the resulting filter function has peaks at 500, 1,500 and 2,500 hertz.

When the laryngeal tone is filtered by such a tube, the resulting resonant peaks will be imposed on the acoustic

OUTPUT SOUND ------>

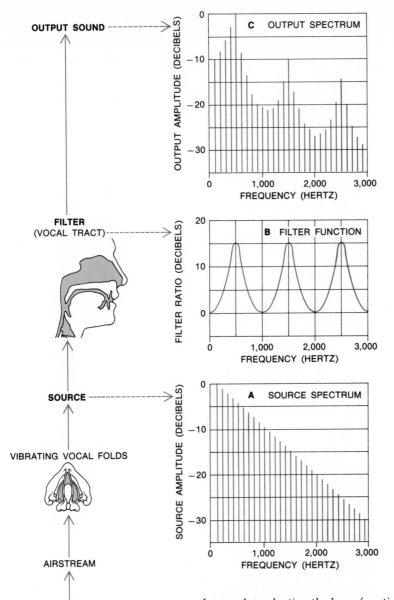

C OUTPUT SPECTRUM

OUTPUT AMPLITUDE (DECIBELS)

0

−10

−20

−30

0   1,000   2,000   3,000
FREQUENCY (HERTZ)

FILTER
(VOCAL TRACT)------>

B FILTER FUNCTION

FILTER RATIO (DECIBELS)

20

10

0

0   1,000   2,000   3,000
FREQUENCY (HERTZ)

SOURCE ------>

A SOURCE SPECTRUM

SOURCE AMPLITUDE (DECIBELS)

0

−10

−20

−30

0   1,000   2,000   3,000
FREQUENCY (HERTZ)

VIBRATING VOCAL FOLDS

AIRSTREAM

LUNGS

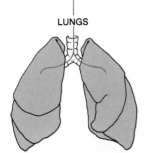

In speech production the lungs function as a power supply, the vibrating vocal folds (cords) as an oscillator and the vocal tract as a resonator. According to the source-filter theory, the source is the laryngeal tone produced when the vibrating vocal folds interrupt the airstream from the lungs. The acoustic spectrum for a source with a fundamental frequency of 100 hertz (A) shows the amplitude decreasing uniformly with frequency. The filter is the vocal tract, which modifies the source in a predictable way. The result is called the filter function. For the vowel [ə] ("schwa"), as in the word "about," the filter function (B) has resonant peaks at 500, 1,500 and 2,500 hertz. When the source is filtered, the resonant peaks are imposed on the output spectrum (C) of the vowel.

41

Fourier Analysis

In 1801 the French mathematician Jean Baptiste Fourier showed it is possible to express periodic functions as the sum of a series of sinusoidal functions. Fourier was not investigating sound at the time (he was interested in the way heat flows through an object), but his theorem can be used to analyze any complex periodic wave, including sound waves.

The drawing illustrates how Fourier analysis would apply to a square wave, such as that produced by some sirens. The component sine waves are on the left, and their sum is on the right; in both, the instantaneous sound pressure is drawn as a function of time. At the top is the fundamental frequency (I). Because a square wave does not have any even-numbered harmonics, the next component is the third harmonic (III): its amplitude is less than that of the fundamental and its frequency three times greater. The next overtone is the fifth harmonic (V): its amplitude is still less than that of the fundamental and its frequency is five times greater. As more overtones are added (VII and IX), their sum, shown on the right, comes closer and closer to a square wave. By adding enough overtones, a square wave can be approximated as closely as is desired.

If the amplitude of each component is plotted as a function of its frequency, as in the illustration on page 41, the resulting graph is called the acoustic spectrum of the wave. Below is a typical speech waveform for a vowel with a fundamental frequency of 100 hertz, as measured by a microphone that is sensitive to variations in air pressure. Because the larynx can change, the laryngeal tone is not perfectly periodic, but it is close enough so that any cycle can be represented as a Fourier sum of a fundamental and its harmonic overtones.

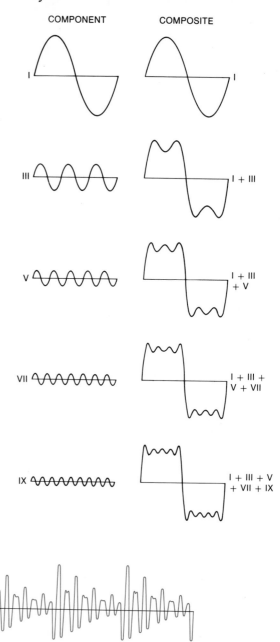

COMPONENT   COMPOSITE

I   I

III   I + III

V   I + III + V

VII   I + III + V + VII

IX   I + III + V + VII + IX

spectrum of the tone. In fact, this filtered spectrum can be produced artificially—either mechanically, with an appropriate sound source and an actual open tube 17 centimeters long, or electronically, by simulating such an acoustic system with a computer. The artificially generated spectrum is similar acoustically to the spoken spectrum, and it sounds like the vowel [ə].

Suppose, however, that a woman had spoken the word "about" and had produced the [ə] at a fundamental frequency of 200 hertz. Then the overtones of the source would be 400 hertz, 600 hertz, 800 hertz and so on. In that case, there would not be any overtones exactly at the resonant frequencies of the vocal tract. The acoustic spectrum of her [ə] would look very much like the man's spectrum, but with every other overtone left out. Actually, because a woman's vocal tract is likely to be slightly shorter than a man's, the resonant frequencies would also be slightly higher, but the general pattern or envelope of the spectrum would be similar. Psychological studies of speech perception have demonstrated that it is this general shape of the spectrum that listeners use to identify which vowel was spoken.

Because the resonant frequencies of the vocal tract are so important for the recognition of vowels, they have been given a special name: they are called formants. The first formant of the vowel [ə] is at 500 hertz, the second formant is at 1,500 hertz and the third formant is at 2,500 hertz. It is these formant frequencies, not the fundamental frequency of the voice, that are essential to intelligible speech. When people sing, they change the fundamental frequency of their voices, but the changes do not affect the formant frequencies and therefore do not affect recognition of the words being sung.

This analysis illustrates, for a single vowel, the modern version of Müller's source-filter theory of speech production. Other vowels are produced by changing the shape of the vocal tract to make it resonate at different frequencies. For example, the vowel [a], which occurs in the first syllable of the English word "father," is produced by moving the tongue down and back in the mouth, which enlarges the mouth cavity and constricts the throat cavity. These

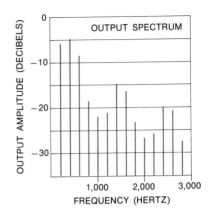

When someone with a high voice says "about" and produces the vowel [ə] at a fundamental frequency of 200 hertz, the output spectrum has no overtones at the resonant frequencies 500, 1,500 and 2,500 hertz. Yet it has the same general shape as the output spectrum for the same vowel when it is produced with a fundamental frequency of 100 hertz (see illustration on page 41), and the vowel has the same phonetic quality.

CROSS SECTION OF VOCAL TRACT　　　MODEL OF VOCAL TRACT　　　ACOUSTIC SPECTRUM

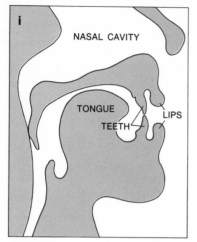

i

NASAL CAVITY

TONGUE

TEETH　　LIPS

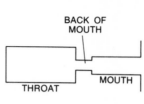

BACK OF
MOUTH

THROAT　　　MOUTH

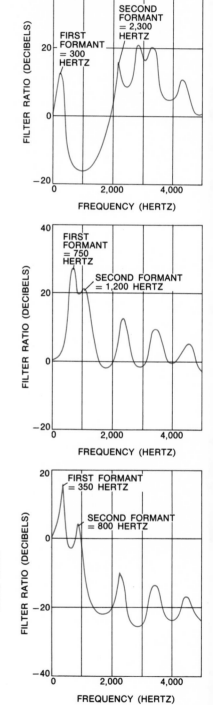

FILTER RATIO (DECIBELS)

FIRST
FORMANT
= 300
HERTZ

SECOND
FORMANT
= 2,300
HERTZ

FREQUENCY (HERTZ)

a

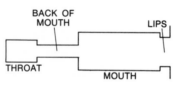

BACK OF
MOUTH　　　　　LIPS

THROAT　　　MOUTH

FILTER RATIO (DECIBELS)

FIRST
FORMANT
= 750
HERTZ

SECOND FORMANT
= 1,200 HERTZ

FREQUENCY (HERTZ)

u

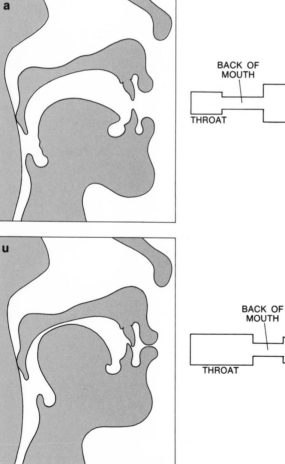

BACK OF
MOUTH　　　LIPS

THROAT　　　MOUTH

FILTER RATIO (DECIBELS)

FIRST FORMANT
= 350 HERTZ

SECOND FORMANT
= 800 HERTZ

FREQUENCY (HERTZ)

changes in shape can be measured precisely from X rays, but their general effect can be approximated by a double tube that is small at the source end and large at the open end. The cross-sectional area of the narrow throat tube should be about one tenth that of the larger mouth tube. Computation of the formant frequencies is more complicated for the double tube, because the two sections are coupled together, but when the calculations are correctly made, the first formant turns out to be about 750 hertz and the second formant about 1,200 hertz if the two tubes are equally long (8.5 centimeters each). These formant frequencies are characteristic of the vowel [a] in natural speech, and artificial vowels generated according to these calculations will be perceived as [a] by listeners.

The vowel [i], which occurs in the word "feet," is produced by just the opposite maneuver of the tongue. For [i] the tongue is moved forward and up, thus enlarging the throat cavity and constricting the mouth cavity. The first two formants for [i] fall at about 300 and 2,300 hertz. The vowel [u], which occurs in the word "boot," is also produced with a high tongue position, but with the tongue drawn

Drawings made from X-ray pictures can be used to estimate cross-sectional areas of the vocal tract, and these estimates can then be used to compute the filter transfer function of the tract. The configurations of the vocal tract for the vowels [i] as in "feet," [a] as in "father" and [u] as in "boot" are depicted at the left, top to bottom. A corresponding model of the vocal tract appears in the center column, and the acoustic spectrum for each vowel is given at the right.

The frequencies of the first two formants of the extreme vowels [a] as in "hot" or "father," [i] as in "heat" or "feet" and [u] as in "hoot" or "boot" relative to the neutral vowel [Λ] as in hut are indicated in the chart at right. (The vowels [ə] and [Λ] are roughly the same sound, except that [Λ] is stressed and [ə] is unstressed.)

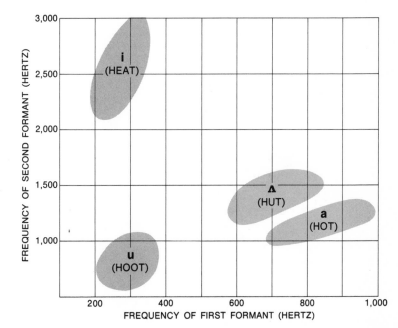

back and with the open end of the vocal tract reduced by constricting the lips. The effect of partially closing the open end of a tube is to lower its resonant frequencies, and the first two formants of [u], therefore, are about 300 and 900 hertz.

We could proceed in this way to correlate the physiological, acoustic and perceptual features of all the English vowels, but this set of four is particularly important. The vowel [ə] can be thought of as the neutral vowel, or point of origin; it is what comes out when we do nothing to alter the resting position of the vocal tract. The vowels [a], [i] and [u] are the most extreme variations from this neutral position that we are able to produce by moving our tongue and lips. All other English vowels are intermediate between these extremes. It is interesting that, although the number of different vowels varies widely from one language to the next, all languages that have been studied have been found to use at least two of these extreme vowels, and most use all three.

The technology, particularly computer programming, that was developed in the course of studying the source-filter theory of human vowel production is quite general. You can

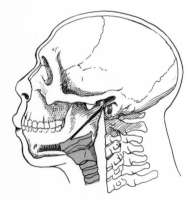
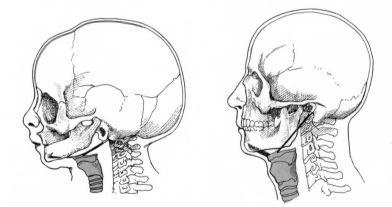

A reconstruction of the larynx (color) in relation to the skull of Neanderthal man (left) shows that it is more similar to that of a newborn infant (center) than it is to that of a modern adult male (right). In Neanderthals and newborn infants the larynx is high and the throat relatively small. Thus neither could produce vowels characteristic of modern languages.

determine the formants for any kind of tube you might be curious about.

For example, from X rays and casts of the vocal tracts of apes, it is possible to compute what sounds they can produce. Apes have a high larynx and a small throat cavity. From estimates of the maximum possible variations in their vocal tracts, it can be shown that it would be impossible for apes to utter [a], [i] and [u].The prediction is said to be supported by the absence of these sounds in recordings of their spontaneous vocalizations. Newborn children are much like apes in this respect. They too have high larynxes and small throats and do not produce [a], [i] or [u] in their earliest cries.

The descent of the larynx into the neck was biologically risky. An elaborate swallowing reflex was required to prevent food from entering the lungs. This change would probably not have occurred if there had been no compensating adaptive advantages. The only advantage known is the increased versatility of the vocal-tract filter, which resulted from the enlargement of the throat.

We can now understand what lay behind the claim that Neanderthals did not possess the capacity for human speech. Their skulls were large, but reconstructions of the skull on top of the backbone suggest that Neanderthals, like apes and newborn children, had short necks, high larynxes and relatively small, immobile throats—that, in short, they could not produce the vowels [a], [i] and [u], which are characteristic of modern human languages. According to this reconstruction and simulation, the variety of vowel sounds that Neanderthals could have produced would not have sufficed for vocal communication anything like the speech of modern man.

This hypothesis has had its critics, but most have focused on possible errors in reconstructing the Neanderthal larynx and throat cavity as if they were more similar to those of newborn than to those of adult human beings. The part of the hypothesis based on the methods of speech science has not been seriously questioned.

According to this hypothesis, Neanderthal man represents an intermediate stage in the evolution of language. His large brain and the archaeological evidence of his level of culture persuade most paleoanthropologists that he must have used some form of vocal communication more sophisticated than the hoots, pants and grunts of living apes, but he would never have been able to speak a modern language. Perhaps his disappearance from the fossil record about 35,000 years ago was a consequence of these limitations, which made him unable to compete successfully with his contemporaries who, like Cro-Magnon man (clearly an early form of *Homo sapiens*), had a modern skeletal structure. If this reconstruction is correct, it provides further support for the claim that human language, as we know it today, was a relatively recent development in the evolution of man.

5
Speech

Although the spelling of part of a word is part of the spelling of that word, the pronunciation of part of a word is generally not part of its pronunciation: if x and y are segments of a word, then Pronunciation(x) + Pronunciation(y) $\neq$ Pronunciation$(x + y)$.

People who are literate in a language that is written alphabetically are educated to think that speaking is like writing, that the speech machinery produces discrete, invariant speech sounds the way a typewriter produces discrete, invariant letters. If their language is English, they know the match of spelling to pronunciation is far from perfect. But the idea that speech does not consist of discrete, invariant segments of sound takes some getting used to.

Analyses made with electroacoustic equipment show that the same speech sound is pronounced differently on different occasions. Some variability is attributable to human fallibility: a speaker cannot do exactly the same thing every time. Some variability is attributable to individual differences: people have slightly different vocal tracts and speak different dialects. These kinds of variability, however, are analogous to differences in styles of type.

There are still other sources of variability that are intrinsic characteristics of speech. Compare the words "key" and "coo." Most people would agree that these words begin with the same consonant sound but end with different vowels. At one level of analysis, this description is correct. At another level, however, the initial consonants of "key" and "coo" are almost as different as the final vowels. Try to pronounce only the initial consonants. In both cases, you raise the back of your tongue against your soft palate, pressure builds up behind it and a plosive sound is made by a small explosion of air when the tongue releases. In one case, this noise is generated in a vocal tract that is already prepared to make the front vowel [i]; in the other, the vocal tract is already prepared for the back vowel [u]. It follows from the source-filter theory that the two explosions must produce different acoustic results. Unless you listen closely you will not notice the difference, because it has no significance in English, but it is unmistakable in an acoustic analysis. Speech sounds are not invariant.

This example also shows that speech sounds are not discrete segments. The vowel that is going to follow is recognizable from the beginning of the preceding consonant; the consonant that preceded is recognizable during the initiation of the following vowel. There is no point at which we can draw a line and say that everything before is pure consonant, everything after pure vowel. Some speech scientists have concluded from such results (of which this is but one example among many) that the appropriate segmental unit for analyzing speech is the syllable, not the speech sound. Each syllable has a vowel; consonants are merely different ways to turn the vowel on and off. When we try to decide where one syllable ends and the next begins, however, the same problems crop up all over again. Speaking flows like dancing; as good dancers take one step, they are already preparing for the next.

Because there is great variability among speech sounds, much of it intrinsic to the way our speech mechanism works, we must ask what it means to say that two speech sounds are the same. What does it mean, for example, to say that the word "peep" has the same initial and final consonant?

If you made a detailed analysis of the articulatory processes and their acoustic results, you could show beyond question that these two consonants are not the same. The initial consonant is accompanied by a small but audible outflow of air, called aspiration, before the vocal folds come together and the laryngeal tone begins for the vowel. The final consonant is not aspirated. (Put the back of your hand

Speech Spectrograms

The sound spectrograph, which was developed at the Bell Telephone Laboratories during the 1940's, is a machine that produces a visible display of the acoustic spectrum as a function of time. Originally, it was hoped the machine would enable deaf people to use the telephone, but this hope was not realized.

In the standard version used in most studies, the acoustic signal to be analyzed is first recorded. Only about two seconds of sound can be analyzed; the two-second recording is played repeatedly. A special kind of paper is wrapped around a cylindrical drum, which makes one rotation every time the recording is played. Each time the drum goes around, the energy in a band of frequencies flows through a stylus and makes a horizontal line; the greater the energy, the more current flows through the stylus and the darker the line that is drawn on the paper.

Each time the drum rotates, the band of frequencies passed by the filter is raised and the stylus is moved upward a corresponding distance on the paper, until a set of parallel lines has been drawn. As the filter moves upward through the frequency range of the signal, therefore, a display is created that shows the changing amounts of acoustic energy at each frequency (the spectrum) as a function of time.

The dynamic range of the writing system is far less than the dynamic range of the human ear. When analyzing speech, therefore, the machine compensates for the decrease in speech energy at the higher frequencies. Two filter bandwidths are available: the wide-band filter (300 hertz) is useful for displaying formants; the narrow-band filter (50 hertz) shows the individual harmonic overtones.

The illustration reproduces one of the first spectrograms ever published. It was made for the phrase "Speech we may see," using frequency compensation and a wide-band filter.

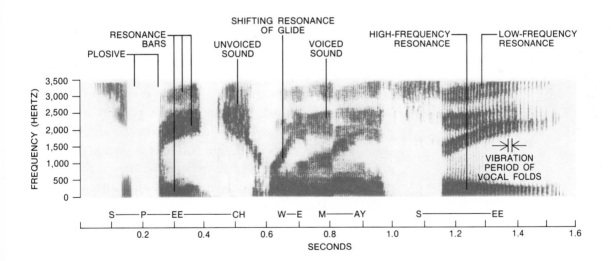

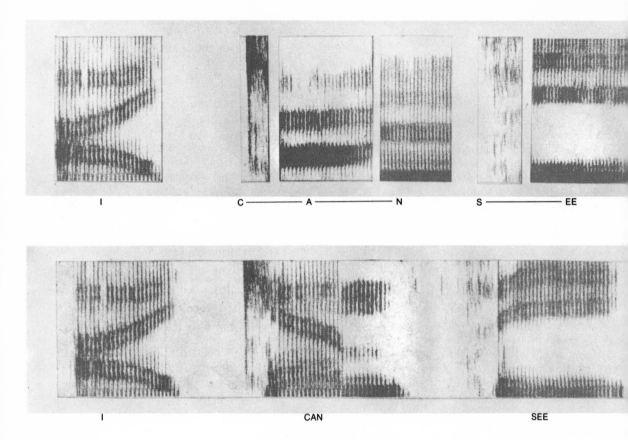

| I | C ——— A ——————— N | S ——————— EE |

| I | CAN | SEE |

near your lips and say "Don't peep now"; you will feel the puff of air for the first "p" but not for the second.) In order to represent this difference, we need two symbols: $[p^h]$ for the aspirated form and $[p^=]$ for the unaspirated. Then we can transcribe the pronunciation of "peep" as $[p^hip^=]$.

For English, this distinction is irrelevant. The aspirated $[p^h]$ occurs only in syllable-initial positions, and the unaspirated $[p^=]$ occurs in all others. There is no pair of words in English that, like $[p^hi]$ and $[p^=i]$, differ only with respect to the occurrence or nonoccurrence of aspiration, because these two speech sounds are not interchangeable in the same position. No confusion can result if we lump them together as the same sound in English. In Chinese, however, aspiration is a distinctive feature; the aspirated and unaspirated forms are different words.

The human vocal tract is not infinitely versatile. It has been estimated that there are less than 30 features of speech

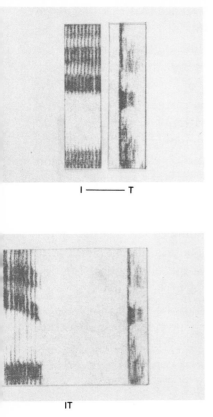

I ——— T

IT

The influence of adjacent sounds in flow of speech is shown by spectrograms of the words "I can see it." In the upper strip the sounds are spoken separately; in the lower strip they are spoken as parts of the sentence.

that can be used distinctively. Each language uses about 10 to 15 of them; no language uses them all. The features used by any particular language are called distinctive features for that language.

I have given an example of a feature, aspiration, that is not distinctive in English. Consider next one that is distinctive: voicing. What is the difference in pronunciation between "veal" [vil] and "feel" [fil]? They are identical except for the initial consonants, and even they are minimally different. For both [v] and [f] the lower lip is brought close to the upper teeth and a noise is made by forcing air between them. The difference is that the vocal folds vibrate while we pronounce [v] but not while we pronounce [f]: we say that [v] is voiced and [f] is voiceless. If voicing were not a distinctive feature in English, [vil] and [fil] would be merely two pronunciations of the same word.

Many other pairs of minimally different words (linguists call them minimal pairs) are distinguishable only on the basis of presence or absence of voicing. Although the difference is obvious to anyone who speaks English, it is the result of a relatively small difference in the manner of production. Whether you say "do" or "too," for example, depends on when your vocal folds start vibrating. In both cases, the flow of air is stopped momentarily and pressure builds up behind the tongue. For "do," the onset of voicing coincides with the release of the stop consonant, whereas for "too," the onset of voicing lags behind the release of the stop consonant about one tenth of a second.

Other languages rely on other distinctions. For example, it is also possible for the onset of voicing to precede the stop release: in Spanish and Dutch the distinctive difference is between coincident and advanced voice onset. The Thai language uses all three: advanced, coincident and delayed voice onsets correspond to three different speech sounds in Thai. All languages in which voicing is distinctive use coincident onset; they differ in whether coincidence is contrasted with advanced or delayed onset or both.

These differences are subtle, in the sense that an adult who has learned to use one set of voice onset times finds it difficult to produce another set when he tries to learn another language. There is some evidence that the difficulty is perceptual; the foreigner cannot hear the distinction he would like to imitate. Up to puberty, children have little trouble with this kind of learning, but then the brain seems to jell, perhaps as a consequence of hormonal effects on the nervous system. Such observations suggest there is a critical period for learning the sound patterns of a language.

One possible application of phonological research would be to simplify and regularize English spelling. In our present orthography, words like "colonel" and "kernel" are pronounced the same way and spelled differently, whereas words like "lead" (the metal) and "lead" (the verb) are spelled the same way and pronounced differently. It has been argued that if we used a phonetic alphabet of about 40 letters, each representing a single speech sound of English, it would be easier for children to learn to read and write, because the written language would be much closer to the spoken language. Although such proposals sound reasonable, they have never been widely accepted, perhaps because libraries are already filled with books written in the existing orthography, because printing machines would have to be changed and (most likely) because people are unwilling to learn new spelling habits.

Not all linguists deplore conventional English orthography, however. Some argue that it is actually very close to an optimal system for representing what a speaker must know about the pronunciation of English words—knowledge that is not predictable by phonological rules. If a person did not know English, simplified spelling would help him read it aloud without comprehension. But people who know English, according to this view, would be required to convert simplified spelling back into something very close to orthography as part of the process of understanding what they were reading.

For example, there is a phonological rule that the plural endings of *rope, robe* and *rose* are pronounced differently. People who speak English know this rule, so it is not necessary to represent the different pronunciations by different spellings; the plural is indicated simply by adding *s*. In a simplified system, these plurals might be written *rowps, rowbz* and *rowzəz*, which could indeed be pronounced correctly by someone who knew nothing more than the rules relating spelling to pronunciation. But people who speak English know that all three endings, when added to nouns, mean "more than one." In order to understand what they were reading, therefore, they would have to convert *-s*, *-z* and *-əz* back into the single underlying concept. If this argument is correct, then learning to read and write conventional English orthography must heighten a person's awareness of significant regularities in the language—regularities that hold for phonetically divergent dialects and are resistant to historical change but are far from obvious in the patterns of sounds we actually utter.

An Alphabet for English Pronunciation

VOWELS				CONSONANTS			
				VOICELESS		VOICED	
i	heed	o	hoed	p pill		b bill	m mill
ɪ	hid	ʊ	hood	t till		d dill	n nil
e	hayed	u	who'd	k kill		g gill	ŋ king
ɛ	head	ɜ	heard	f feel		v veal	
æ	had	ʌ	but	θ thigh		ð thy	l lip
a	hod	ə	about	s sue		z zoo	r rip
ɔ	hawed			š Confucian		ž confusion	y yet
				č chaw		ǰ jaw	
				ʍ whale		w wail	
				h hale			

English pronunciation can be represented reasonably well by a phonetic alphabet that has 13 symbols for vowels and 25 for consonants. When this alphabet is used, the sentence "In the beginning was the word," for example, is written ɪn ðə bəgɪnɪŋ wʌz ðə wɜrd.

Because this alphabet represents only those features that are distinctive for speakers of English, it cannot be used to transcribe speech in another language.

In any case, it is clear from what has been said that even phonetic spelling cannot be an accurate description of the physiological processes or the acoustic results of speaking. Phonetic transcriptions represent speech sounds by discrete, invariant letters. We have seen that the process of speaking is not a series of staccato jumps from one fixed position to the next, that the stream of speech cannot be cut up into discrete sounds.

What, then, is the relation of a phonetic transcription to actual speech?

Imagine a machine with a keyboard into which we can type a sequence of phonetic symbols. The machine produces a sequence of speech sounds corresponding to what we have typed. If the machine contained nothing but a tape recording of each speech sound of English, plus a mechanism for switching rapidly from one sound to the next, its output would be unintelligible.

If the machine could be made to introduce the appropriate transition between every possible pair of speech sounds, its output might be intelligible, but it would still sound unnatural. We could improve the output, however, if we gave the machine a description of the human vocal tract and enabled it to treat each typed symbol as a package of features for controlling the successive configurations of the tract, subject to all the normal physiological limitations of that system. Then, instead of playing prerecorded segments of speech, the machine could generate its own speech, as a human speaker would.

If the machine is to generate its own speech signal, however, we will have to type in not only the sequence of speech sounds but also information about the pitch of the laryngeal tone, the location of stress in the utterance and the rate of speaking. In short, if the machine is to speak naturally, it will have to be a very sophisticated machine with a detailed input transcription. One way to characterize the research program of speech science is as an attempt to discover all the information that would be required to build and program such a speaking machine.

It may seem odd that a highly sophisticated machine is needed to do something that people do so easily. However, it is not the machine we are interested in but what it can teach us about how people speak. For example, experiments with these machines (called computer-implemented vocal-tract models) have already taught us that people prefer to use speech sounds that can be generated by imprecise articulatory movements.

There are certain configurations of the vocal tract that are optimal, in the sense that they can be perturbed through a considerable range with no significant effects on the acoustic output. These configurations correspond to the sounds people prefer to use in speaking. The extreme vowels [a], [i] and [u] are examples. Optimal consonant positions are also stable. For example, [t] is formed by bringing the blade of the tongue against the gum ridge, obstructing the vocal tract and creating two tubes, one about 12 centimeters long and the other about five centimeters long. By computer-implemented vocal-tract modeling it can be shown that a high resonance of the back tube and the first resonance of the front tube coincide when the obstruction occurs at this point; minor perturbations in the location of the obstruction do not seriously affect the acoustic result. There are six stable points at which the tract can be obstructed, and each corresponds to a place of articulation that is used to produce consonants in some language (though not all are used in any one language). The choice of these optimal points of articulation, therefore, is universal, regardless of language, because they depend on the shared physiology and acoustics of the human vocal tract. The only choice open to speakers of any language is which of the limited number of true consonantal positions they will decide to use.

In English, for example, three optimal points are chosen for the stop consonants [p], [t] and [k]. The labial articulation of [p] results in very low resonant frequencies; the dental articulation of [t] results in relatively high resonant frequencies; the velar (soft palate) articulation of [k] results in intermediate resonant frequencies. The choice of these three points of articulation is optimal, not only in the sense that all three can be produced with relatively imprecise articulatory movements but also in the sense that these three produce clearly distinguishable acoustic results.

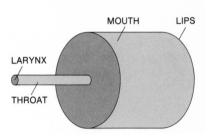

A simple two-tube model illustrates the vocal-tract configuration for the vowel [a]. Although the throat tube has only one tenth the cross-sectional area of the mouth tube, both will resonate at frequencies corresponding to quarter wavelengths. If both are 8.5 centimeters long, therefore, both will resonate at the same frequency (about 1,000 hertz). Due to coupling (interaction between the tubes), however, one resonance will be slightly higher than the other. Small variations in the lengths of the tubes will merely change which tube gives the lower resonance and which tube gives the higher, a change that will not affect the sound of the vowel. Consequently, the filtering characteristic of the tubes is very stable.

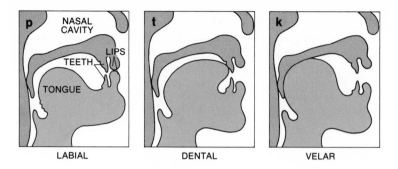

LABIAL   DENTAL   VELAR

Sketches show vocal-tract configurations for the labial, dental and velar points of articulation used to produce the stop consonants [p], [t] *and* [k].

In the light of these facts, consider again what it means to call two speech sounds the same. It cannot mean that they are produced with the same configuration or movement of the vocal tract. The acoustic analysis explains what has long been known from X-ray data, which show that people make the same sounds with different articulatory maneuvers.

We call two speech sounds the same because they sound alike. In order to speak intelligibly, it is necessary to utter the correct sounds, but what is "correct" depends much more on our hearing than on our feeling for the motor movements that produce the sounds. That is one reason it is so difficult for congenitally deaf people to learn to speak.

It would seem, therefore, that a phonetic transcription is not as much a description of the speaker's vocal behavior as it is a representation of the sounds produced. We will return to the perception of speech in chapter 6, but first we should consider some properties of speech that cannot be localized in particular segments of the utterance.

Take pitch, for example. The perceived pitch of our voice, high or low, depends on the frequency of vibration of the vocal folds. If the vocal folds are going to vibrate, they must have some frequency of vibration. They could vibrate at a constant frequency, but such a monotone would not merely be unnatural, it would make it difficult to tell when one sentence ended and the next began. Variation in pitch of the voice carries significant information that is not easily represented by a sequence of discrete speech sounds.

There are three lengths of utterance within which pitch changes can convey information: syllables, words and sentences. Sometimes the three lengths coincide, as they do when we utter the monosyllabic sentence "No," but when we take examples in which they differ, we discover that they follow different rules.

In many tonal languages, syllables must be pronounced with different pitch contours. The Peking dialect of Chinese, for example, has four tones: flat, rising, falling-rising and falling. The same syllable means different things depending on which tone is used. For example, *mā* (with the level tone) can mean "mother," *má* (rising tone) can mean "hemp," *mǎ* (falling-rising tone) can mean "horse" and *mà* (falling tone) can mean "scold." In the Peking dialect, pitch is a distinctive feature, just as voicing is a distinctive feature in English. Voicing, however, is a feature of individual sounds, whereas pitch is a feature of whole syllables.

At the word level, pitch contributes to the stress pattern. We tend to think that a stressed syllable is slightly louder than the others, but the pitch change is probably more important. The larynx works in such a way that, unless special efforts are made to avoid it, a rise in subglottal air pressure will produce a simultaneous rise in the loudness and pitch of the laryngeal tone. When we stress the first syllable of a polysyllabic word like telegraph, the pitch of that syllable is normally higher than the pitch of the others.

The rules for assigning stress to the syllables of long words in English are complicated. Consider, for example, that in "telegraph" the main stress is on the first syllable, in "telegraphy" it is on the second and in "telegraphic" it is on the third. In order to assign the correct pitch contour to such words, a speaker must know far more than how to form the individual phonetic segments. In some cases, he must know whether the word is a noun or a verb: in the sentence "Will they convict the convict?" the verb "convict" receives stress on the second syllable but the noun on the first. Assigning words to the categories "noun" or "verb" raises questions of syntax that fall outside the limits of phonological theory. For that reason, some linguists claim it is a mistake to think of phonology and syntax as two autonomous levels of description; they prefer to think of them together as closely related components of grammar.

At the level of sentences, assignment of a pitch contour

depends on still more complex considerations. Speakers generally try to fit a sentence or a clause into a single breath. (To do this, a speaker must have some idea how long his sentence is going to be before he starts to speak it.) Because air is expelled from the lungs as we talk, it takes a little extra effort to produce a rising pitch toward the end of a breath group; the easy way is to let the pitch fall at the end of the sentence. Then the beginning of the next sentence can be signaled by its higher pitch. This pattern is not universal, of course, but the boundaries of sentences are so important that some clear signal must be given to show where they occur.

In English, a rising pitch at the end of a sentence usually signals a particular kind of question. For example, if "John ate it all" is spoken with a falling pitch contour, it makes an assertion; if it is spoken with rising pitch, however, it asks a question. The difference between declarative and interrogative sentences is a matter of syntax, so these facts might be viewed as another argument that syntax and phonology are not independent. But declarative and interrogative sentences are normally used to perform different speech acts—acts of asserting or acts of questioning. What pitch contour a speaker uses tells us something about his intentions in uttering particular words on a particular occasion.

Pitch contours also depend on what the speaker thinks his audience already knows. Stress (and higher pitch) usually go with new information. For example, a person who asks "What did Mary bring?" already knows that Mary brought something, so in the answer "She brought a cake" it is the new information, "cake," that receives stress. Characterizing what a speaker thinks a hearer knows at any given time goes beyond the bounds usually set for a theory of phonology.

Acoustic analysis of speech forces attention to the many respects in which the speech signal differs from alphabetic writing. It also forces attention to acoustic differences between speech sounds that listeners ignore because the differences are not significant in their language. How people are able to hear those features that are significant and ignore differences that are not significant poses a central question for any theory of speech perception.

6

Speech Perception

Traces of our evolutionary history are plain enough in our vocalizations. Evolution has also left its mark on our auditory system, but there the evidence is less direct. Our ears are far more versatile than our tongues.

The human ear is a major undeclared asset of the telecommunication industry; it can dig a message out of the most degraded kind of signal. If it could not—if high fidelity were required for accurate speech perception—voice communication would be far more expensive than it presently is. Indeed, if Mr. Watson's ears had not been able to understand low-grade speech, Alexander Graham Bell would not have invented the telephone when he did.

Imagine the following experimental situation. In one room a person reads aloud a prepared list of syllables, words or sentences. His voice is picked up by a microphone and transduced into electric signals that pass through a voice-communication system to a second room, where they are transduced back into sounds that are heard by a group of listeners. The listeners write down what they think the speaker said. At the end of the test, their papers are collected and scored against the materials the speaker read. This experimental procedure was invented in the 1920's at the Bell Telephone Laboratories. It was called an articulation test, because researchers used it to estimate how well a telephone could "articulate" the sounds of speech.

In one form or another, the articulation test is still the basic method for studying speech perception. In experiments, one aspect of the test situation is varied, and all

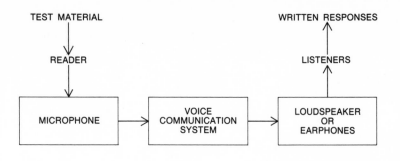

Flowchart indicates the sequence of steps in the articulation test, the basic method for studying speech perception. The test material, or message, is recoded several times. It begins in a written form, is recoded as acoustic waves by the reader and then is transduced into electric currents by the microphone. The electric signal may be modified in various ways by the communication system before the loudspeaker or the earphones transduce it back into acoustic waves, which listeners then recode in written form. The signal changes constantly, but if no errors occur, the message is kept unchanged.

others remain constant; differences in the percentage of sounds heard correctly indicate the effect of the variation.

Researchers have been marvelously ingenious in adapting the articulation test to their needs. Consider some of the aspects of speech perception that can be studied. Different test materials can be compared to see whether some kinds of messages are easier to hear than others. Different speakers can be compared, or a machine that synthesizes artificial speech can be substituted for a human talker. If the communication system includes a recorder and playback, the speech can be uttered at one time and its intelligibility tested later, or the speech rate can be slowed down or speeded up. The loudness of the speech can be varied, its waveform can be distorted in various ways, filters can be used to study the relative importance of different bands of frequencies, echoes can be introduced and the speech can be mixed with different kinds and amounts of noise. Different listeners can be compared, as they are when the effects of hearing loss are measured, or listeners can be given various expectations about the message, either explicitly or by repeated exposure to it. The scoring can be the simple percentage correct, or the particular confusions that occur can be tabulated in matrixes. The list of variables that can be (and have been) explored goes on and on.

It was clear from the earliest tests that speech is highly resilient. As long as speech is audible, changes in its intensity have no effect on intelligibility until it gets so loud it hurts. Conversation is possible as long as there is as much energy in the speech signal as in a masking noise; serious difficulty is not encountered until the noise power is about four times as great as the speech power; that is to say, the signal-to-noise ratio is −6 decibels. If the speech waveform is turned into a square wave by peak clipping, it is still intelligible—in fact, it sounds very crisp, because clipping off the high-amplitude peaks makes the consonants as loud as the vowels. Other mutilations destroy any vestige of naturalness, but naturalness is not important for intelligibility. Rapid interruptions and echoes are annoying but have relatively little effect on intelligibility. Speeding or slowing by a factor of two does not affect the accuracy of speech perception.

All this resistance to noise and distortion is remarkable, because many of the things we can do to speech with modern electronic equipment are totally novel. Speech could not possibly have evolved its present form in order to resist degradations that never existed before.

Results obtained with filtered speech put the case as clearly as any. When a high-pass filter allowed listeners to hear only those frequencies in the speech above 1,900 hertz (about an octave below the top of the piano keyboard), 67 percent of the nonsense syllables used in the tests could still

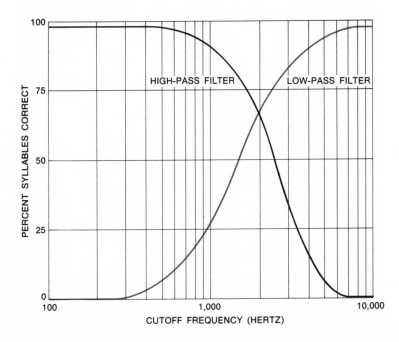

Articulation-test scores for nonsense syllables are plotted as a function of cutoff frequencies of high-pass and low-pass filters. With a high-pass filter that allows listeners to hear only frequencies above 1,900 hertz, 90 percent of nonsense syllables are heard correctly; with a low-pass filter that allows listeners to hear only frequencies below 1,000 hertz, just 27 percent are heard correctly. The curves cross at 1,900 hertz, where 67 percent of syllables are heard correctly.

be identified correctly. (Under conditions where 67 percent of nonsense material like *dack, plutt, rabe, swoot, thope* can be heard, meaningful sentences like "China is industrializing rapidly" can be heard almost perfectly.) There was nothing peculiar about the frequencies above 1,900 hertz, however, because when a low-pass filter allowed listeners to hear only the frequencies below 1,900 hertz, they did equally well. Apparently, not much information is carried by frequencies below 400 or above 5,000 hertz, but within these limits no particular portion of the speech spectrum is crucial for speech perception.

What should we conclude from such observations? Three things. First, intelligibility does not depend on naturalness. Second, the cues that are used to identify speech sounds must be broadly represented in the speech signal, because we can throw away large portions of the signal without making it unintelligible. Third, our ears need no special training in order to make good use of any scraps of information that are left. Taken together, these three conclusions suggest a hypothesis—namely, that the human auditory system has evolved special perceptual mechanisms for detecting and decoding speech cues.

The broad distribution of speech cues was implied in our discussion of speech production. In chapter 5 we saw that they were distributed in time: in words like "key" and "coo" the vowel is prefigured in the consonant and the consonant perseverates in the vowel. If we think of this interaction in terms of speech perception instead of speech production, we can ask whether the human ear is particularly sensitive to these transitions between speech sounds. There is evidence that it is. We also saw in chapter 4 that information is distributed broadly in frequency: the laryngeal tone is rich in harmonics. When the laryngeal tone starts or stops, the change is signaled by the appearance or disappearance of harmonically related overtones throughout the speech spectrum. Therefore, voice onset times should be very dependable perceptual cues. Moreover, changes in the frequency of any harmonic indicate changes in the pitch contour, which is an important indicator of word and sentence shapes.

These broad and distinctive patterns are examples of

speech cues. It has proved surprisingly difficult to build machines that can recognize these complex, dynamic cues, but they leap out at us when we listen to speech. Have we evolved a special speech decoder, a neurophysiological system that processes speech differently from other sounds?

Consider some evidence in favor of this hypothesis. Take lateralization of function. Speech production and perception are localized in the left hemisphere of the brain of nearly everyone. Now, suppose we speak pairs of different syllables simultaneously into the two ears of a listener. Each ear is connected to the left and right hemispheres, but the pathway from the right ear to the left hemisphere is bigger (has more fibers) than the pathway from the right ear to the right hemisphere. Because the right ear reports more strongly to the speech hemisphere, it is not surprising that the listener is more accurate in reporting what was said to his right ear. On the other hand, if we present pairs of simple melodies instead of spoken syllables, we get the opposite result: the left ear, which reports predominantly to the nonspeech hemisphere, hears melodies better than the right ear. The right-ear advantage for speech and the left-ear advantage for music indicate that these two kinds of signals are processed on opposite sides of the brain—speech in the left hemisphere, music in the right. That is to say, there appears to be a part of the adult human brain that is specialized for hearing speech.

To determine what cues our speech perception center is attuned to, we need to have precise control over the speech sounds. We need to vary particular aspects of speech in controlled ways to determine which variations sound like speech cues and which do not. This kind of control is now possible with computer-implemented vocal-tract models, but most of what we know about speech cues was learned with a cruder device, the Pattern Playback.

With the Pattern Playback it is possible to draw any kind of picture and then hear what it sounds like. Most pictures sound like futuristic music. You can make it sound like speech, however, if you copy the picture carefully from a speech spectrogram. Then the problem is to explore which particular parts of the spectrogram you must copy in order

The Pattern Playback

The Pattern Playback, which was developed and used by the Haskins Laboratories during the 1950's, is an optical scanning device that converts a sound spectrogram back into sound. The Haskins Laboratories, founded by Caryl P. Haskins, is a private research organization. It became interested in speech science when it tried to develop devices that would read text aloud to blind people, devices that would identify letters or letter groups and generate distinctive sounds. Many sound alphabets had been tried, but none was found that could be understood faster than the dots and dashes of Morse code. (Morse code cannot be understood at speeds greater than one tenth that of human speech.) The Haskins group decided that only a reading machine that produced speechlike sounds would permit a tolerable rate of information transmission. The Pattern

Playback was developed to explore the kind of signals a reading machine would have to generate if its output were to sound like speech.

The Playback worked on the principle of a player piano. A speech spectrogram was printed on a large transparent sheet, the sheet was drawn past a row of photocells and the output of the photocells was used to control the intensity of the harmonics of a complex tone of fixed frequency. Speech reproduced in this way was intelligible, although the monotone pitch sounded unnatural. The Playback enabled experimenters to convert hand-drawn spectrographic patterns into sound and to search for aspects of the pattern that are essential for speech perception. One of the first hand-drawn spectrograms is shown, along with the speech spectrogram from which it was drawn.

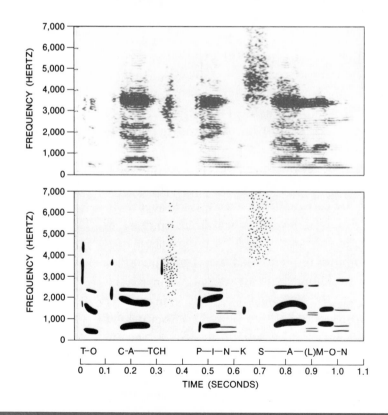

to preserve the speechlike quality. After you have omitted everything that is not essential, you are left with a picture of the basic acoustic cues for speech perception.

For example, a speech spectrogram will show three or four formants of the vowels. Which ones are most important? By drawing all possible combinations of formants and listening to the results, it can be shown that only the first and second formants are essential. Vowels sound more natural with the first three, but they are perfectly distinguishable without the third.

Experiments with consonants confirm the importance for perception of the transition between the consonant and the following vowel. From listening tests it is possible to determine the simplest spectrograms that will be perceived as the voiced stops [b], [d] and [g] in front of the vowels [i], [a] and [u]. The transitions that are heard as the same consonant are different for different vowels; for [di] and [du], for example, a rising and a falling transition are both heard as the same speech sound. The important thing is where the transition comes from, not which way it goes. One reason it is possible to get information so rapidly from speech signals is that the cues for successive speech sounds overlap. This overlap would seem to make the signal more complicated, but the human listener has no trouble with it.

Compare the simplified spectrograms for [ba], [da] and [ga]. The only difference is the transition into the second formant; the transition to the first formant is the same in all three. This fact suggests an experiment. You might draw a series of spectrograms in which everything is the same except the slope of the transition into the second formant of [a]; vary the slope in small steps over a wide range; play these spectrograms in random order and ask listeners which ones they hear as [ba], [da] or [ga]. Because the transitions can be drawn much steeper than any transitions a human speaker could make, listeners could not have heard them before, yet they will agree in identifying the synthetic sounds: steeply rising transitions are [ba] and steeply falling are [ga]. Flat or slightly rising transitions are [da].

Listeners have relatively sharp categories for these three consonants. If they are given pairs of syllables differing in

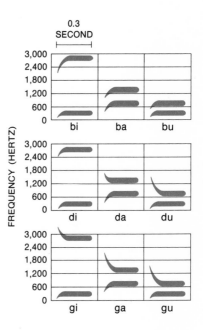

When synthetic spectrograms using information in the first and second formants are played on the Pattern Playback, they are heard as the voiced stop consonants [b], [d] and [g] followed by vowels [i], [a] and [u].

the slope of transition and asked whether they are the same or different, a difference will not be reported unless the two syllables happen to fall into different categories. Within a category, all transitions sound alike.

Now, repeat these experiments, but this time omit everything that was held constant in the first experiment: do not draw the first formant, the second formant or the transition into the first formant. All that the listeners will hear are the different transitions into the second formant. Although in an appropriate context these transitions are perceived as consonants, in isolation they are not heard as spoken sounds but simply as rising or falling chirps. If too much of the speech spectrogram is omitted, the listener no longer hears the sounds in the speech mode. Moreover, when listeners are given pairs of chirps and asked whether they are the same or different, they cannot hear differences that were perfectly obvious in the first experiment. There are no categories in human speech processing for chirps.

Speech perception, therefore, is different from the perception of other sounds, even other sounds that are very similar acoustically. When listening to speech, we do not

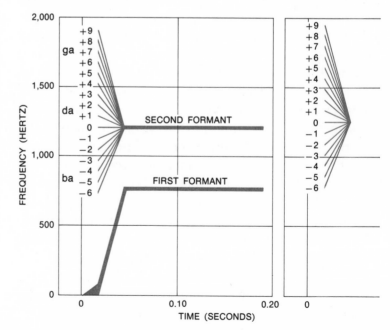

The transition between a consonant and the vowel that follows it is important for speech perception. At right is a schema for a series of stop consonants differing only in second-formant transitions. When the stop consonants are played on the Pattern Playback, they are heard as [ba], [da] or [ga] as the transitions change over a range of slopes that are assigned numbers from −6 to +9 (left of diagram). When only transitions are played (right of diagram), they are heard not as speech sounds but as ascending or descending "chirps."

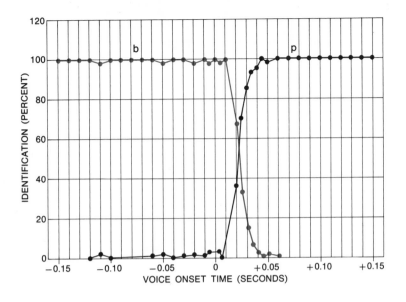

If the onset of voicing (vibration of the vocal folds) precedes or coincides with the release of a stop consonant, English speakers will hear it as a voiced consonant; if the onset lags the release by 0.02 second or more, it will be heard as a voiceless consonant. Each negative value represents 0.01 second before release of the consonant; each positive value, 0.01 second after release of the consonant. When voice onset time is less than +0.03 second, the consonant is heard as [b]; when voice onset time is more than +0.03 second, as [p]. At about +0.02 second, the crossover occurs: [b] turns into [p]. Small differences in onset time are not heard unless they fall at category boundary.

hear auditory events, such as rising or falling pitch glides, but speech: we hear [ba], [da] or [ga]. Such observations provide further evidence that our perception of these sounds is accomplished by a processor that is specialized for dealing with speech.

Similar results can be obtained by varying the voice onset time. If the onset of voicing is delayed in small steps, there comes a time (at about 0.02 second) when [b] turns into [p]. Once again, small differences in onset time are not heard unless they fall at the category boundary; within a category, all onset times sound alike.

Some speech scientists believe that the speech mode of perception is innate, the result of a special evolutionary adaptation for speech. It has been shown, for example, that frogs have a special detector that responds only to small objects that move across its visual field at particular rates. Human beings, these scientists argue, are born with similar detectors for speech cues. Their critics reply that the detector might be acquired through learning, because different languages select different features as significant. Then the question becomes whether people are born with an innate ability to learn such distinctions. We will return to this question in chapter 10.

The experimental dissection of spoken syllables has taught us much about speech perception. In everyday life, however, we seldom hear monosyllables in isolation. We speak and hear longer strings of words in what we like to think are grammatical sentences. Is the perception of a sentence nothing more than the perception of a sequence of syllables? Or are there relations between syllables that are just as important as the transitional effects between individual speech sounds?

It is possible to conduct articulation tests with sentences. For example, we can construct a large set of sentences all having the same number of content words: *"Peat is cut in bogs and used for fuel," "White snow fell on the dark fields," "Jane sat on the broad back porch"* and so on. What listeners write down can be scored either for the number of complete sentences or for the number of individual content words they heard correctly. Then, for comparison, we can construct word lists that use these same content words in haphazard order: "fell, bogs, broad, Jane, peat" and so on. If both types of test material are presented in enough noise to ensure that listeners will make mistakes, we can compare the scores obtained for words heard in sentences with the scores obtained for those same words heard in isolation.

The results show clearly that words are easier to hear when they are used in sentences than when they are spoken in isolation. Because words are spoken more rapidly (and probably less distinctly) in sentences, and because listeners have to remember five of them at a time, all the obvious mechanical advantages are on the side of the isolated words. Nevertheless, the sentence context provides cues that make the words much easier to hear.

In this case, however, the cues are not acoustic. They have something to do with what listeners expect to hear. For example, if you hear "Peat is cut in the bogs and used (mumble)," the antecedent context helps you guess what the mumble was. You expect something like "as bricks," "to burn," "for fuel." With these expectations, even the slightest acoustic hint can determine your choice.

This hypothesis can be tested in another experiment. Suppose you tell listeners in advance that they are going to hear one or the other of two words—for example, either "tree" or "boy." All they have to decide is which one they heard. With this advance information, people can hear "tree" and "boy" correctly 95 percent of the time under noise conditions where, if all they knew was that they would hear English monosyllabic words, "tree" and "boy" would be heard correctly only 5 percent of the time. Less acoustic information is needed to select one out of two alternatives than to select one out of 1,000 or more. Speech perception—indeed, perception generally—is much more accurate when you know what to expect.

Words are easier to hear in sentences than in isolation, therefore, because the context gives you a better idea what to expect. In order to pursue this kind of perceptual cue, however, we must go beyond acoustic analysis. Expectations are in a listener's mind, not in the acoustic signal.

At this point, therefore, I must interrupt my story in order to develop some basic ideas required to discuss language at a different level of abstraction. As long as I was discussing speech, there were reasonably concrete physical and physiological processes to talk about. In order to probe what is going on in a person's mind, however, a more indirect approach is required.

7

The Structure of Language

Ask the average person what language is, and he will probably answer in terms of the social and personal uses it serves: a language is a set of symbolic conventions adopted by a social group for the purpose of communicating ideas, expressing emotions, enlisting cooperation, providing entertainment—the list of particular functions served is not predictable, but most people will include the expression and communication of ideas.

This answer is perfectly correct, but note that there is something unusual about it. Suppose you ask the same person what walking is. He will probably not tell you it is a method of locomotion adopted for the purpose of going to the store, getting exercise, accompanying friends, carrying packages or whatever. Instead, he will probably think of the parts of the body involved in walking and the processes those parts carry out: walking is something you do with your legs and feet; it consists of putting one foot forward, shifting the weight onto it, then putting the other foot forward and so on.

This answer is perfectly correct, too, but it is a different kind of answer. Note that we could give the second kind of answer to the question, What is language? Language is something you do with words; it consists of uttering one word, then another word, then another and so on. And this answer would be perfectly correct, too.

We need to sort out at least three kinds of answers that we could give to the question, What is language? First, we could give an answer in terms of structure: a language is a set of sequences of words. Second, we could give an answer in terms of process: a language is the set of skills that enables a person to utter and understand those sequences of words. Third, we could give an answer in terms of use: a language is a set of social conventions for using those skills in uttering those sequences of words in order to achieve particular ends.

There is an order to these three answers. The third answer presupposes the second, and the second presupposes the first. This order would seem to dictate a logical order of exposition: first structure, followed by process and finally use. However regrettable it may seem, this logical order has already been violated: the relatively mechanical processes of speaking have already been discussed. I cannot go on that way, however. Before I can discuss the more abstract mental processes involved in speaking and understanding speech, I must first sketch out at least briefly the basic structure of the conceptual system on which those mental processes operate.

Let us turn, therefore, to structure.

The most obvious structural feature of human language is that it consists of sequences—sometimes long sequences—of symbols. The first question to ask, therefore, is why this should be the case.

In order to focus on sequencing, it will be helpful to consider a signaling system that is simpler than any human language, yet incorporates this sequential feature. Imagine a device that can produce only two different signals. Call them 0 and 1. If these signals are the total vocabulary of the device, it will be able to label only two things. Its vocabulary can be increased, however, if it can produce these atomic signals in pairs: 00, 01, 10 and 11 give the device labels for four things. If it can produce the two signals in triplets, eight things can be given different labels: 000, 001, 010, 011, 100, 101, 110 and 111. The longer the sequence, the larger the vocabulary. With n-tuples, there can be 2^n different labels. The general rule is m different atomic signals in sequences of length n provide m^n different labels.

Because the potential size of the vocabulary increases exponentially as the length of the sequences increases lin-

An Artificial Language

Natural languages are complicated. A scientist who wants to understand some particular aspect of language may try to simplify the task by constructing an artificial language incorporating that aspect in an abstract, idealized form. The following is the first of three illustrations of this strategy of linguistic research.

Imagine a communication system that uses only two symbols, 0 and 1. Whenever 0 occurs, the system goes into state S_0; whenever 1 occurs, the system goes into state S_1. When the system is in state S_0, the next symbol must always be a 1. In state S_1, however, the system has a choice: it chooses 0 with a probability of 0.2 and it chooses 1 with a probability of 0.8. This system will generate messages like 1110101111110111 . . . , strings of 1's punctuated by occasional occurrences of a single 0.

This communication system can be described in a state diagram:

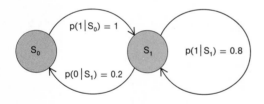

where the circles are states and the arrows are possible transitions between states. Whenever an arrow is traversed, a symbol is added to the message. Each arrow is labeled with the probability of a given symbol in a given state.

Alternatively, the system can be described by rules of message formation:

R1.	$S_0 \rightarrow 1\ S_1$	WITH PROBABILITY 1.0
R2.	$S_1 \rightarrow 1\ S_1$	WITH PROBABILITY 0.8
R3.	$S_1 \rightarrow 0\ S_0$	WITH PROBABILITY 0.2

where the term on the left is the state that the system is in and the terms on the right are the symbol that occurs and the state that the system goes to next. For example, if the system starts in state S_0, it might continue as follows:

S_0	STARTING STATE
1 S_1	BY RULE R1
1 1 S_1	BY RULE R2
1 1 1 S_1	BY RULE R2
1 1 1 0 S_0	BY RULE R3
1 1 1 0 1 S_1	BY RULE R1

and so on. This message can also be represented by a tree diagram:

and so on. The "growing point" of the tree is always on the right.

If we think of 1 as standing for any letter of the alphabet and 0 as the space between words, this system provides a reasonably good model for sequences of letters and spaces in written English.

early, sequencing is an efficient way to achieve a large vocabulary with a limited number of different atomic signals. Sequencing is, in fact, the way all human languages do it. That is why an ability to produce different sequences of signals and respond differently to them is so important for speaking and understanding a human language.

In fact, the sequential strategy is so powerful that all human languages make double use of it. The various speech sounds in the language can be arranged in different sequences to form thousands of different words, which illustrates the first use of the sequential principle. The second use occurs when these thousands of words in the vocabulary are arranged in different sequences to form an enormous variety of different sentences. (It could be argued that there is still a third use: these sentences can be arranged in different orders to tell different stories. How we arrange sequences of sentences, however, has less to do with the structure of language than with the story we want to tell, so for the moment we will concentrate on the first two uses of the sequential principle.)

It takes longer to produce a sequence of n signals than to produce one signal; the price for using a sequential strategy is the additional time it takes. If a sequentially organized signaling system is to be efficient, therefore, the signals should be brief and should follow each other in rapid succession. In conversational English the average word has about five phones, or sounds; when we speak at a rate of 150 words per minute, we are producing individual sounds at a rate of 12.5 per second. Similar computations for other languages give comparable estimates. This rate of information output may seem slow in comparison with high-speed computers, but it is orders of magnitude faster than the rate at which other animals can signal. Indeed, even human beings cannot communicate that rapidly with any signaling system other than speech. Moreover, a rate of 150 words per minute leaves a good margin of safety, because speech can be speeded up by a factor of two (or even three) and still be intelligible. Apparently the human capacity for speech has evolved in a way that not only exploits the sequential principle but that does so at very rapid rates.

The faster we go, of course, the greater is the likelihood that we will make a mistake. The possibility of error limits the use of the sequential principle. If we use it fully (as we do with sequences of integers in arithmetic), then every sequence of atomic signals is meaningful, and a mistake simply converts one significant sequence into another; the receiver has no way to tell when he has gotten the wrong message. If we want to permit the recognition (and, sometimes, the correction) of mistakes, therefore, we cannot use all possible sequences. Communication engineers use the term redundancy to describe the unnecessary repetition of words that occurs when the sequential principle is not fully exploited. Redundancy means that the sequences we do use will be longer than they have to be.

Human language is obviously redundant by this definition. It is not possible for us to pronounce all conceivable sequences of speech sounds. This point can be illustrated in terms of written English. With an alphabet of 26 letters, there are 26 possible one-letter words, 676 possible two-letter words, 17,576 possible three-letter words and 456,976 possible four-letter words. If we used no more than four letters per word, therefore, we could have a total vocabulary of 475,254 different words, or about the number in *Webster's New International Dictionary*. The longest words in the dictionary, however, have many more than four letters. It has been estimated that if some language could use a maximally efficient spelling system, its books would be about one half the length of ours. But such a system would mean that sequences like *xdse, xdsf* or *tqsz* would all be meaningful words.

The same situation exists at the second level: not every sequence of words forms an intelligible sentence. Although we can pronounce a string of words like "Cattle sabertooth gas drench incapacity," we give it a list intonation, not a sentence intonation, because these words clearly do not form a sentence. It has been estimated that if some language could use all possible sequences of letters to form words and all possible sequences of words to form sentences, its books would be about one quarter the length of ours. By this criterion, 75 percent of what we write is redundant.

This kind of redundancy is not a total waste, however, because it provides an insurance policy against noise. It is because we know some sequences of words are inadmissible that we can hear words more accurately in sentences than in isolation.

The question is, How do we know which sequences are admissible?

At the first level, we memorize the admissible sequences. It is not quite that simple, because every language has rules for word formation; in English, for example, we can recognize things like "administrativeness" or "affirmativity" as possible words, even though we may never have seen them before (neither is in *Webster's New Collegiate Dictionary*). In general, however, knowing which sequences are words is a matter of rote memory.

At the second level of sequencing, memorization is out of the question. There are too many possible sentences. For example, it has been estimated that each successive word is, on the average, chosen from 10 alternatives possible in that context. (This estimate may be too low, but a larger number would make the argument even stronger.) This means there are about 10^{10} grammatical sentences 10 words long. Because there are less than 3.16×10^9 seconds per century, we would not have time to memorize all of the admissible 10-word sentences, even if we could work at a rate of one second per sentence. And even if we could, we would know only the 10-word sentences, which are a trivial fraction of all the sentences we would need to know.

We do not need to look at children, therefore, to realize that they could not possibly be learning to produce and understand sentences by memorizing the sentences they hear. We must assume they are building some kind of language engine in their heads that will enable them to generate admissible sequences of words. A grammar is a linguist's set of design specifications for that engine. The grammar is a structural specification in the sense that it does not describe how the engine must work or what it can be used for but only what it must accomplish if the person who runs it is to be able to use his language to communicate with others. A person who has built such an engine can use it to

A Measure of Information

In 1948 Claude Shannon, then at the Bell Telephone Laboratories, published "A Mathematical Theory of Communication," in which he developed a theory of selective information and applied it to the design of communication systems and other information-processing systems. At the foundation of that theory was a rationale for measuring the amount of information in a message.

The unit of measurement is the *bit* (short for binary digit), which is the amount of information required to select one from among two equally probable alternative messages. For example, the choice of a message from among eight equally probable alternatives requires three bits of information: the first bit narrows the choice from one of eight to one of four equally probable alternatives; the second bit narrows it from four to two alternatives; the third selects the desired message from the remaining two alternatives. The general formula is $2^H = N$, where H is the measure of information in bits and N is the number of equally probable alternatives.

According to this formula, the selection of a letter from a 27-character alphabet (26 letters and a space) requires 4.7 bits of information, because $2^{4.7} = 27$. In written English, however, the 27 characters are not all used with equal probability. The space is used most often, followed by *e, t, o, a, i, n, s* and so on. Moreover, the probability of a given letter depends on the letters that have preceded it: *u* is very probable following *inq* but very improbable following *til*. Unequal probabilities reduce the average amount of information per letter below 4.7 bits. Shannon estimated that the number of bits per letter in written English is somewhere between 0.6 and 1.3. That is to say, in some contexts many different letters can follow, but in other contexts only one letter is possible; on the average, it works out to about two equally probable alternatives.

These figures can be used to estimate how many different sentences of any given length can occur in written English. In order to be as conservative as possible, take Shannon's lower bound, 0.6 bit per letter. The average word length is about 5.5 characters (4.5 letters plus a space), so the number of bits per word is, on the average, 5.5×0.6, or 3.3. Because $2^{3.3} = 10$, the amount of information per word encoded in written English is equivalent to the amount that could be encoded if we used only 10 words, each of which occurred with equal probability in all contexts. Given 10 alternatives per word, a five-word sentence would be selected from $10 \times 10 \times 10 \times 10 \times 10$—or 10^5—alternative sentences, a 10-word sentence from 10^{10} alternatives and so on. Even with this conservative estimate, the number of sentences is seen to be enormous—far more than anyone would speak or hear in a lifetime.

EQUAL PROBABILITIES

MES-SAGE	CODING TREE	CODE	PROB-ABILITY	BITS	$p \times H$
A		00	$\frac{1}{4}$	2	0.5
B		01	$\frac{1}{4}$	2	0.5
C		10	$\frac{1}{4}$	2	0.5
D		11	$\frac{1}{4}$	2	0.5
					2.0 BITS

UNEQUAL PROBABILITIES

MES-SAGE	CODING TREE	CODE	PROB-ABILITY	BITS	$p \times H$
A		0	$\frac{1}{2}$	1	0.50
B		10	$\frac{1}{4}$	2	0.50
C		110	$\frac{1}{8}$	3	0.375
D		111	$\frac{1}{8}$	3	0.375
					1.750 BITS

produce admissible sequences of words. If he encounters any sequence his engine cannot generate, he knows there has been a mistake; either the sequence is wrong or there is something wrong with his language engine.

Linguists phrase their design specifications in terms of syntactic rules that the language engine must conform to. In chapter 8 we take a look at how such rules can be formulated. Here we simply wish to point out some implications of looking at language in this way.

This view of language emphasizes its creative aspects. Sometimes we deliberately quote sentences we have heard before, and sometimes we use polite clichés to facilitate a conversation, but most of the sentences we utter are created as we utter them. If our sentence is longer than seven or eight words, moreover, there are so many different possible sentences that the chances are good we are doing something that has never been done before.

According to this view, it is necessary to distinguish clearly between a person's speech and his language, between what he does and what he knows how to do. His language includes an enormous variety of possible sentences, most of which he will never hear or utter. His speech, on the other hand, includes only that particular set of sentences he creates and utters during the course of his life. One of the deep psychological mysteries of language is how a person, on the basis of exposure to a limited sample of speech, manages to build a language engine able to produce and interpret an unlimited variety of sentences.

This distinction between speech and language is not accepted by all students of human communication. In particular, some psychologists argue that observable behavior provides the only objective evidence on which to construct a science and that mentalistic claims about what a person knows, means, remembers, thinks or expects are at best speculative hypotheses and at worst religious superstitions. In this case, the observable behavior is speech. If "language" refers to anything at all, these psychologists say, it must refer to the total record of the speech behavior of a particular social group. Throughout this book, however, I have assumed that "language" is a valid scientific concept and that a science of language should explain what people know how to do, not merely what they actually do. Their speech behavior is simply one important source of evidence about what they are able to do, about their capacity for and knowledge of language.

By providing only the design specifications a language engine must meet, not the processes it must perform in order to meet them, a grammarian can avoid responsibility for describing the actual neurophysiological mechanisms of speech. A computing machine that could meet his structural specifications would be just as good an instantiation of his grammatical theory as a human brain and vocal tract would be. This degree of abstraction has both advantages and disadvantages. It enables grammarians to define their own universe of discourse and adopt their own criteria of evidence; linguistics is not a branch of neurophysiology. On the other hand, it is sometimes difficult for scientists who approach language in a different way to understand the implications of grammatical theories for their own research (and vice versa).

According to a structural view, a language is a (possibly infinite) set of sentences and a grammar is an abstract specification of how to identify all and only sequences of words that are sentences. The central concern is with formal structures that distinguish grammatical from ungrammatical sequences and with structural relations between different types of sentences.

As we have seen, structuralism is not the only conception of language that we could imagine, but it is the one that has received the most detailed analysis. In the course of this analysis, it has become apparent that there are many different ways to approach the problem. In order to choose among them, various criteria have been suggested. One is simplicity. If two grammars generate the same set of sentences (and structural descriptions) but one is simpler than the other, the simpler grammar is to be preferred. But simplicity must be qualified by plausibility. If two grammars generate the same set of sentences but the processes required to implement one are more plausible psychologically than those required to implement the other, the more plausible grammar is to be preferred. Both simplicity and plausibility are unfortunately vague, and sometimes the two seem to conflict.

I began this chapter with a structural answer to the question, What is language? The only interesting way to characterize the sets of grammatical word sequences that can form a language is in terms of rules for identifying admissible grammatical sequences. Before I can go on to consider what kind of language engine in our heads might follow those rules, however, I need a more explicit account of what such rules might look like. For that I must turn next to syntactic theory.

8
Syntax

O f all the subjects studied at school, grammar is the one children like least. Modern theories of syntax are more like algebra than traditional grammar was. But then, most children are not very fond of algebra either.

One reason people dislike grammar is that they are required to learn a lot of technical terms they see no need for. There is no way to discuss the syntactic component of grammar without this terminology, but at least we can hope to understand why it is necessary.

Consider the problem we face. We are given the set of all possible sequences of words and asked to formulate a set of rules to identify all and only those sequences that form sentences. Because sentences are uttered and heard one word at a time, we might consider rules like this: Rule 0 includes a list of all the words that can begin a sentence. It tells us that if we choose word w_i, we must go next to Rule w_i, which includes a list of all the words that can follow w_i. If we choose word w_j from this second list, we must go next to Rule w_iw_j, which includes a list of all the words that can follow the pair w_iw_j. And so on.

It is easy to see what is wrong with this strategy. It requires us to write a new rule for every admissible initial sequence of words. Thus, we end up with more rules than there are grammatical sentences. We would do better simply to list all the grammatical sentences. But that is no theory at all—that is just the set of facts we want a theory to describe.

How can we reduce the number of rules? One way is to

sort the words into categories. Then we can state the rules in terms of sequences of categories instead of sequences of words. Rule 0 would now include a list of all the categories of words that can begin a sentence. If we choose a word from category c_i, we must go next to Rule c_i, which includes a list of all the categories that follow any word from category c_i. And so on.

This new strategy looks more promising, because there are fewer admissible sequences of categories than there are admissible sequences of words. Historically, this was the first strategy adopted by linguists. The categories were called parts of speech, and each category received its own name. In English, the usual categories are noun, verb, adjective, adverb, preposition, pronoun, conjunction, article. In careful work, these categories are further divided into subcategories: proper noun, count noun, mass noun and so on. Learning these names has distressed children ever since, but the theoretical advantage of stating rules in terms of categories instead of words is too great to resist.

Do all languages have the same parts of speech? The list just given is characteristic of the classical Indo-European languages, but the details are not applicable to languages having different grammatical structures. Most linguists assume the distinction between nouns and verbs is universal, at least in the sense that there will be nominal expressions to indicate what is being talked about and verbal expressions to indicate what is being predicated of it. But critics have cited languages like Nootka as counterexamples. In Nootka, a Wakashan language spoken by American Indians living on Vancouver Island, any word (any stem) can be used either nominally or verbally by adding appropriate affixes to it. In such languages, it would be necessary to look for rules governing the admissible sequences of affixes rather than the admissible sequences of parts of speech. Even here, however, the general principle would be the same: categorizing the elements that can occur reduces the number of rules required. Therefore, I will illustrate the principle with examples familiar to English-speaking readers.

One advantage of using categories to state the rules is that such use also categorizes sentences. For example, "The boy read a book," "A farmer killed the hawk," "The wind rustled the leaves" and many other sentences are all instances of the sentence category defined by the sequence Article + Noun + Verb + Article + Noun.

Linguists quickly realized that there are category sequences worth naming that are shorter than a whole sentence. For example, in the sequence Article + Noun + Verb + Article + Noun the sub-sequence Article + Noun occurs twice. Let this sub-sequence be called a noun phrase (NP). Then this category of sentence can be defined as Noun Phrase + Verb + Noun Phrase.

SENTENCE				
NOUN PHRASE		VERB PHRASE		
NOUN PHRASE		VERB	NOUN PHRASE	
ARTICLE	NOUN	VERB	ARTICLE	NOUN
THE	BOY	READ	A	BOOK
A	FARMER	KILLED	THE	HAWK
THE	WIND	RUSTLED	THE	LEAVES

The internal structure of a sentence is clear when the parts of the sentence are summarized in table form.

The virtue of isolating and naming sub-sequences in this way is not that it shortens the specification for this particular category of sentence but that it begins to take account of the internal structure of the sentence. Let the sub-sequence Verb + Noun Phrase be called a verb phrase (VP)—for reasons to be noted in a moment. Then the syntactic structure of this category of sentence can be summarized in a table, where the different categories we have just adopted are lined up under one another: the category Sentence is first divided into two constituents, Noun Phrase + Verb Phrase; the category verb phrase is divided into two constituents, Verb + Noun Phrase; the two noun phrases are then divided into the constituents Article + Noun. Finally, words from each category can be inserted in place of category names to give a pronounceable sentence.

There is a surprising variety of ways to represent this structural information. It can be given as an outline:

Sentence (s)	*The boy read a book*
Noun Phrase (NP)	*the boy*
Article (ART)	*the*
Noun (N)	*boy*
Verb Phrase (VP)	*read a book*
Verb (V)	*read*
Noun Phrase (NP)	*a book*
Article (ART)	*a*
Noun (N)	*book*

Alternatively, it can be represented in a tree graph. Or it can be represented by the use of parenthetical brackets; each bracket has a subscript to indicate its category:

$$[_{s}[_{NP}[_{ART}the]\ [_{N}boy]]\ [_{VP}[_{V}read]\ [_{NP}[_{ART}a]\ [_{N}book]]]].$$

These different representations all say the same thing; they are merely notational variants.

If we remember our grammar-school lessons, we will recognize that the procedure we have just gone through is called parsing the sentence. The resultant structural information is called the phrase structure of the sentence. Note that anomalous sentences like "The wind killed a book"

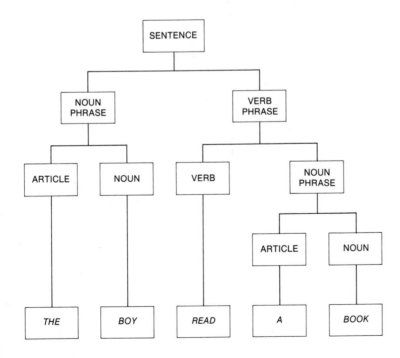

The phrase structure of the sentence "The boy read a book" is represented by a tree graph with labeled nodes.

85

also have this phrase structure; it is difficult to assign any clear interpretation to such sentences, but the fact that they are meaningless (if they are) does not mean that they are ungrammatical. Syntax cannot do everything.

With this example of a syntactic structure before us, the next problem is to formulate syntactic rules for it. Once again, there are many notational variants, but we will use rewriting rules:

Rule 1: s → NP + VP
Rule 2: VP → V + NP
Rule 3: NP → ART + N

The arrow means that the symbol on the left "can be rewritten as" the symbols on the right. Assume s is given. Then we can apply Rule 1 to rewrite s as NP + VP. Next we can apply Rule 2 to VP to obtain NP + [V + NP]. And finally we can apply Rule 3 to the two NP's to obtain [ART + N] + [V + [ART + N]]. There are no rules for rewriting any of these symbols, so the process terminates at this point, and lexical insertion begins. The phrase structure is simply a record of which rewriting rules were applied and what they were applied to.

The syntactic notions "subject" and "object" can be defined in terms of the phrase structure. The subject of a sentence is the NP that is immediately dominated by s, and the object of the verb is the NP that is immediately dominated by VP. (Note that if we had not introduced VP to designate the sequence V + NP, these simple definitions would not be possible.) Subject and object are structure-dependent categories; which NP is which depends on where it occurs in the phrase structure of the sentence.

This formal definition of subject and object is correct for English, in which the order of declarative sentences is always subject-verb-object (svo), but would have to be revised for vso languages (like Hebrew, Welsh or Berber) or for sov languages (like Japanese, Turkish or Hindi). The universal rule seems to be that the subject noun phrase always precedes the object noun phrase; the three known types of languages result from having the verb come first, between or last in declarative sentences. For each type of language, however, subject and object would be defined as structure-dependent categories.

We have now built up considerable theoretical machinery and terminology for discussing a very simple example. The effort would be useless, however, if Rules 1–3 were needed only for this one sentence structure. It is critically important—it is, indeed, a major test of the descriptive adequacy of a grammar—that these same rules be required to describe many other kinds of sentence structure. I will not attempt to prove here that this is in fact the case, but if you were to examine a variety of other sentences, you would find repeated need for these three rules. And, of course, you would also have to formulate other rules like them; Rules 1–3 are only a tiny (but important) fragment of English syntax.

For example, Rules 1–3 characterize only sentences with transitive verbs. It is easy to add Rule 4, $\text{VP} \rightarrow \text{V}$, in order to characterize sentences like "John slept," which have intransitive verbs. In analyzing VP, there would then be a choice between Rule 2 and Rule 4. This choice can be represented by combining both rules into one:

$$\text{Rule 2: } \text{VP} \rightarrow \text{V}(+ \text{NP}),$$

where the parentheses indicate that the NP is optional.

Let us not lose sight of why we need this structural description. We want some way to identify all and only the sequences of words that are sentences in a language. To accomplish that, we must specify some properties that sentences have and nonsentences do not. What we find is that in order to describe a sentence, we have to give not only the sequence of words but also the phrase structure—the words plus a phrase-structure tree or labeled bracketing. It must be possible for the syntactic rules to associate a phrase structure with any grammatical sequence of words.

I have now suggested in brief outline what linguists mean when they talk about phrase-structure grammar. The important question that remains is whether a phrase-structure grammar can identify all and only the grammatical sentences in any human language. The answer is not entirely clear. No one has yet succeeded for English, but no one is trying very hard. What happened was that when linguists tried to write phrase-structure grammars that would deal with a variety of sentences, they discovered that they had to write different rules for very similar sentences and that in doing so they failed to characterize some obvious intuitive relations between sentences.

For example, the structure of the sentence "What book is the boy reading?" is somehow related to the structure of the sentence "The boy is reading a book." It would be possible to write a phrase-structure grammar that would accept both of these sentences, using one set of rewriting rules for interrogative sentences and another set for declarative sentences, but there would be no way to indicate that the sentences are structurally related. In order to capture such syntactic relations, linguists have supplemented rewriting rules with transformational rules. The introduction of syntactic transformations was proposed by Zellig S. Harris of the University of Pennsylvania, but Noam Chomsky of Massachusetts Institute of Technology has done the most to develop that proposal. With the addition of transformational rules, the grammar has two components: a base component (the phrase-structure rules) and a transformational component (the transformational rules).

Rewriting rules operate on a syntactic category to give other categories, whereas transformational rules operate on a phrase structure to give other phrase structures. For example, no serious modification of Rules 1–3 would be required for them to give the phrase structure:

[[the boy] + [is] + [reading + [what book]]],

where "is" is an auxiliary verb and "what" is an interrogative adjective. Something like this would be required for the declarative sentence, and we can obtain the interrogative sentence from the underlying structure by applying two transformational rules. The first transformation would move "what book" to the beginning of the sentence, giving:

[[what book] + [[the boy] + [is] + [reading + [0]]]],

where "0" is null. ("0" indicates the gap left after moving "what book.") The second transformation would invert the subject, "the boy," and the auxiliary verb, "is," giving:

[[what book] + [is] + [[the boy] + [0] + [reading + [0]]]].

Transformational rules are very powerful. In order not to

abuse them it is necessary to show that they are needed elsewhere and are not introduced arbitrarily just to rescue a theory from one sticky problem. In this case, the Wh-Fronting transformation is required for all questions with "what," "who," "where," "when," "which," "why" or "how" and for such nominalizations as "what book the boy is reading" in "I know what book the boy is reading." The Aux Inversion transformation is required for such yes-no questions as "Is the boy reading a book?"

Only two kinds of transformations are generally allowed. One kind, like Wh-Fronting and Aux Inversion, changes the order of constituents. A second kind deletes constituents; for example, "Mary ate lunch and John ate lunch" is transformed by deletion of the first "ate lunch" into "Mary and John ate lunch." Both kinds are structure dependent. That is to say, all syntactic transformations must include a description of the class of phrase structures they can be applied to, as well as a description of the change (movement, deletion) they introduce.

Note that syntax is not a description of the psychological or neurophysiological processes that occur when sentences are spoken or understood. It is simply an attempt to characterize as precisely as possible what sentences are; it does not attempt to say how they are realized when people speak. In particular, no claim is made that rewriting rules or transformations correspond to mental processes going on in the heads of language users. The rules describe what people know, not what they do.

Although transformational rules can greatly simplify the formulation of a grammar, they have had a stormy history in linguistic theory. At one time the set of transformational rules was extremely complex, because there seemed no other way to capture many obvious relations. Some theorists even used transformations to characterize semantic as well as syntactic relations between sentences. Then it was observed that any theory allowing the unconstrained use of transformational rules is equivalent in power to a universal Turing machine. Because a universal Turing machine is a hypothetical computer that can compute any computable function, this means the syntax of any language can be

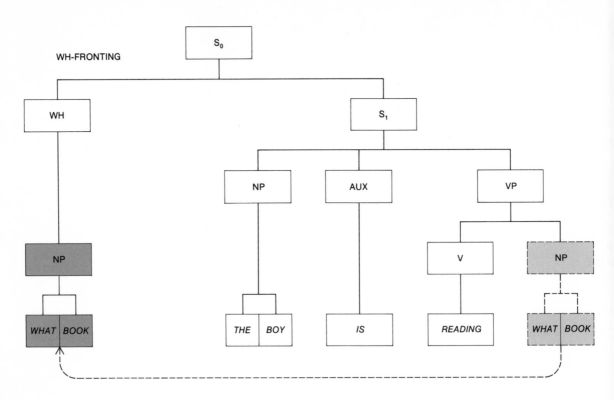

WH-FRONTING

formulated in terms of transformational rules (not just natural languages but also artificial languages, such as those used in mathematics, logic or computer programming). In order to make empirically interesting claims about the syntax of natural languages, therefore, it is necessary to constrain the kinds of transformations that will be allowed and to offer plausible grounds for the particular constraints that are proposed.

The transformational component of a grammar can be constrained in many different ways. For example, the number of constituents involved in any transformation might be limited, or particular descriptions of structures that transformations can apply to might be specified, or a single transformation might be allowed to carry out only a single structural change (only movement or only deletion), or undesired results of transformations might be filtered out and rejected by special constraints. The theoretical possibilities are so various that it is difficult to know which approach to take.

Syntactic transformations can lift a constituent out of the original phrase structure of the sentence and attach it elsewhere, thus generating new phrase structures. The Wh-Fronting transformation (above) is required for questions beginning with "what," "who," "where," "when," "which," "why" or "how"; the Aux Inversion (opposite page) is required for yes-no questions. According to some views, each transformation leaves behind a residue, or trace, that marks where the moved constituent came from, making it possible to "remember" the original sentence structure.

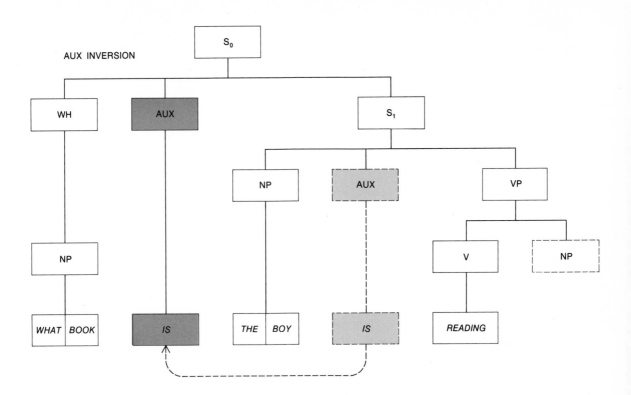

At this point, consideration of the mental processes implied by different kinds of constraints may be helpful. For example, it might be possible to develop a restricted list of types of transformations; perhaps all languages have similar base components, but different languages make different choices among a limited number of transformation types. If descriptively adequate grammars could be written without using any transformations not on the list, we might ask whether there are any psychological grounds for accepting such a restricted list. Would more-complex transformations overload a speaker's information-processing capacity? Are people innately prepared to appreciate some transformations and not others? Would more-complex transformations be impossible for children to learn?

This approach would parallel that taken in phonology, where there is a restricted list of distinctive features of speech sounds, and each language exploits a different subset of those features. In the case of phonology, anatomical and neurophysiological reasons can often be given for restricting

A Second Artificial Language

Imagine a communication system that uses only two symbols, 0 and 1. An admissible message consists of any string of 0's followed by exactly the same number of 1's:

```
0 1
0 0 1 1
0 0 0 1 1 1
0 0 0 0 1 1 1 1
```

and so on. All other strings are inadmissible.

If we try to describe this system by a state diagram, it will look like this:

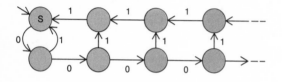

Any path starting and ending at state s will generate an admissible message. Note, however, that because there is no limit to the length of admissible messages, there can be no limit to the number of states.

The system can be described very simply by rules of formation, however. Only two rules are needed:

> R1. S → 0 S 1
> R2. S → 0 1

The arrow means that the symbol on the left can be rewritten as the string of symbols on the right. For example:

S	STARTING STATE
0 S 1	BY RULE R1
0 0 S 1 1	BY RULE R1
0 0 0 1 1 1	BY RULE R2

At this point the system must stop, because it does not have a rule for rewriting any of the symbols in this terminal string. This message can be represented by a tree diagram that indicates its internal structure:

The "growing point" of this tree is always in the middle of the string.

A grammar of English must include rules like R1. If we think of 0 as a left parenthesis and 1 as a right parenthesis, the system described provides a model for some strings of parentheses: ( ), (( )), ((( ))) and so on. (A better model for parentheses would add the rule s → s s.)

Now, English allows sentences to be embedded parenthetically inside sentences:

> The girl is here.
> The boy who said (the girl is here) is here.
> The man who said (the boy who said (the girl is here) is here) is here.

And so on. Speakers of English do not use such self-embedded sentences because they are so difficult to understand. Because there is no grammatical rule that prohibits them, however, Noam Chomsky used the possibility of such parenthetical constructions to argue that English cannot be a "finite state" language; that is, the set of grammatical English sentences cannot be generated by a system whose state diagram has a finite number of states. A system at least as powerful as a phrase-structure grammar is required.

A Third Artificial Language

Imagine a communication system that uses only two symbols, 0 and 1. An admissible message consists of any string of 0's and 1's, followed by that same string a second time:

```
0 0
1 1
0 0 0 0
0 1 0 1
1 0 1 0
1 1 1 1
0 0 0 0 0 0
0 0 1 0 0 1
```

and so on. All other strings are inadmissible.

Suppose we try to describe this system by rewriting rules. We might begin with the rules:

```
R1.  S → 0 S
R2.  S → 1 S
R3.  S → T
```

These rules are obviously not sufficient, but rules R1 and R2 will generate a first string of 0's and 1's. This first string will end when rule R3 introduces T. At that point we will need rules that will generate exactly the same string a second time. How should those rules be phrased?

Obviously, the system must have some memory of what it did the first time if it is going to do the same thing again. One way to describe that memory is to use context-sensitive rules:

```
R4.  T → 0     IN THE CONTEXT 0 —
R5.  T → 1     IN THE CONTEXT 1 —
R6.  T → 0 0   IN THE CONTEXT 0 0 —
R7.  T → 0 1   IN THE CONTEXT 0 1 —
```

and so on. Because there is no limit to the length of the first string, however, there will be no limit to the number of context-sensitive rules needed to rewrite T correctly. There will be as many rules for rewriting T as there are admissible strings, so this solution is no improvement on a simple list of the admissible strings. One solution is to use a different kind of rule. Let x represent any string. Then we can add to rules R1–R3 the following transformational rule:

> T1. STRUCTURAL DESCRIPTION: X T
> TRANSFORMATION: 1 2 ⇒ 1 1

The top line describes the structure to which the bottom line applies: if you have any string (term 1) followed by T (term 2), transform it into term 1 followed by term 1.

Rule T1 is more powerful than a rewriting rule that applies to a single term, because T1 applies to a whole string. For example, to generate 0101:

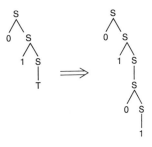

A transformational rule applies to a phrase structure to generate a new phrase structure.

English allows such constructions as "Tom, Dick and Harry were born in Seattle, Chicago and Boston, respectively," where the order of terms in the second sequence must follow the order chosen in the first sequence. Noam Chomsky used the possibility of such constructions to argue that English cannot be a phrase-structure language; its grammar must include transformations as well as simple rewriting rules.

the list of possible features. Perhaps, in the case of syntax, comparable psychological reasons could be found for restricting the list of possible transformation types.

Questions like the above can be answered only by careful analysis of the mental processes that occur when people produce and understand sentences. Structural analysis of the set of grammatical sentences is not sufficient, by itself, to determine a unique theoretical result. That is to say, transformational rules are so powerful that they permit a variety of descriptively adequate grammatical theories. In order to select among the alternatives, data about psychological processes should supplement data about grammatical structure.

Psychologically, the significant feature of transformational rules is that they are structure dependent. Consider the sentence "Is the boy reading a book?" Suppose that the Aux Inversion transformation that derives this sentence from "The boy is reading a book" was not structure dependent, but instead was stated as follows: Find the first word in that sentence that is a member of the category Auxiliary Verb and move it to the front of the sentence. This rule would work for the example just described. But now apply it to the sentence "The boy who is sitting on the porch is reading a book." The result is a nonsentence: "Is the boy who sitting on the porch is reading a book?" In order to find the right auxiliary verb to move, the rule must be stated in terms of the subject of the main clause ("The boy . . . is reading the book"), and both "main clause" and "subject of" are defined in terms of the structure of the sentence.

A language-processing system must operate on syntactic structures, not on unstructured sequences of words. This fact has important theoretical implications. For example, at the close of chapter 6 it was noted that words heard in sentences are easier to recognize than the same words heard in isolation. The sentence context helps a listener narrow the set of possible alternatives among which he must discriminate. Someone who had not considered syntax might suppose that this narrowing is accomplished on purely probabilistic grounds: some sequences of words occur much more frequently than other sequences do, and a listener learns those probabilities and uses them to make his guesses. This explanation, however, ignores the fact that a language-processing system operates on syntactic structures, not on unstructured sequences of words. What a listener knows are the rules of grammar, not the probabilities of sequences.

If we are to explain how people understand speech, therefore, we must explain how their knowledge of grammatical rules is represented and used. We can get an idea of what such an explanation would look like if we consider how computers have been programmed to parse sentences. In general, mechanical parsing systems proceed word by word through a sentence, looking up the syntactic categories of the words, checking sequences of categories against the sequences allowed by the rules and assigning appropriate phrase structures to the sequences. It is not difficult for a computer to parse simple sentences, but sentences involving syntactic transformations pose more of a challenge.

Consider, for example, how a mechanical parsing system might deal with the sentence "What book is the boy reading?" Presumably, the system would recognize that the noun phrase "what book" had been moved from its underlying position; the phrase would therefore be held in a temporary memory buffer until its underlying position could be determined. Because "read" is a transitive verb, the only possible gap in this sentence for a noun phrase would occur after "reading." Therefore, the system could determine that "what book" is the object of this verb. If we asked the system to parse "What book is the boy reading the newspaper," it would not find a gap into which "what book" could fit, and therefore it would (correctly) reject that sequence of words as a nonsentence.

The details of such a scheme can be worked out in various ways, but the general idea is that a fronted noun phrase has to be remembered temporarily until an appropriate gap is found for it and its grammatical function can be determined. Presumably, a human listener must also remember it, just as a mechanical parsing system does.

How could such a hypothesis be tested? One way makes use of sentence pairs like the following:

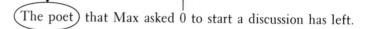

The poet that Max asked 0 to start a discussion has left.

The poet that Max tried to start a discussion with 0 has left.

In each sentence "0" indicates the place from which the noun phrase, "the poet," has been moved. These sentences can be presented to experimental subjects; comprehension can be tested by such questions as "Who asked whom to do what?" or "Who tried to do what with whom?"

Augmented Transition Networks

Efforts to program computers to respond appropriately to information expressed in a natural language have led to the development of automatic parsing programs. Augmented Transition Networks (ATN) illustrate one strategy for writing such programs. Any sentence that can be analyzed by phrase-structure rules can be recognized by an ATN system.

An ATN system based on Rules 1–3 described in the text is shown in the diagram. Corresponding to each rule is a network of states connected by arcs: the top network tries to recognize sentences (s), the middle network tries to recognize verb phrases (VP) and the bottom network tries to recognize noun phrases (NP). Four kinds of arc are shown: (1) SEEK arcs allow a state transition only if a phrase of the type named on the arc has been found, so control is transferred to the network designed to recognize that type of phrase, (2) CAT arcs allow a state transition only if the word being scanned belongs to the category named on the arc, (3) JUMP arcs allow a state transition without advancing the input sequence of words, (4) unlabeled arcs leaving one state without entering another signify that the network has accepted the string of words and that control is transferred elsewhere.

For example, if the input sequence of words is "the boy read a book," the system will start in state s_0 and try to recognize it as a sentence. The first arc transfers control to state NP_0, which accepts "the boy" as a noun phrase and assigns it as subject before returning control to state s_1. The next arc transfers control to state VP_0, which identifies "read" as a verb, then transfers control to NP_0, which accepts "a book" as a noun phrase, assigns it as object, then transfers control back to VP_2, which accepts "read a book" as a verb phrase and transfers control back to s_2, which accepts "the boy read a book" as a sentence.

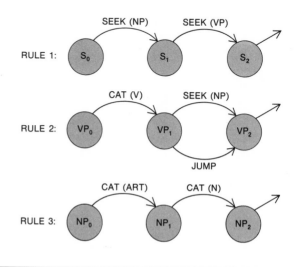

Now, suppose that the presentation of these sentences is interrupted immediately after the words "to start" and an unrelated memory task is imposed, after which the sentence presentation resumes. In the first sentence, when this interruption occurs the person will already have found the gap into which "the poet" fits and will no longer be holding it in memory. In the second sentence, when the interruption occurs the person will not yet have found the gap and will be remembering it at the same time he is asked to remember unrelated information. The interruption causes more trouble for the second sentence than for the first, both in remembering the unrelated information and in answering the comprehension question. Apparently the two memory tasks interfere with each other. This result supports the hypothesis that people, like mechanical parsing systems, really do hold a displaced noun phrase in short-term memory until they find the place in the sentence structure where it originated and in that way determine its underlying syntactic function.

This example illustrates how the mental processes involved in understanding sentences can be explored experimentally. Much work remains to be done, however, before such experiments will yield the kind of information needed to decide between alternative ways of restricting the transformational component.

As soon as we begin to consider the mental processes involved in speaking and understanding sentences, however, it becomes difficult to limit our attention solely to syntactic structures. A syntactic processor must work in close harmony with a lexical processor that provides information about the particular words that are spoken.

9
Lexicon

The lexicon for any given language is all the words (or, to use the technical term, lexemes) in that language. Different languages have different lexicons, not only because they use different spoken noises to express similar meanings but also because they express different meanings. What concepts a language has words for depends on what the people who speak it like to think and talk about. The way people talk and the way they think are closely related. Any speech community has considerable latitude for shaping its lexicon to its own convenience and to its own habitual patterns of thought.

Perhaps that way of saying it is misleading. If you are a member of a particular speech community, you are not free like Humpty-Dumpty to make words mean whatever you want them to mean. If you don't use words the same way other people do, they won't understand you. Some linguists—Benjamin Lee Whorf is probably the most widely read—have argued that our habitual patterns of thought are shaped by the words our society has agreed to use. People who live in very different societies live in different worlds, not merely in the same world with different labels attached to things. People cut up nature and think about it as they do, Whorf said, not because those categories and concepts are necessarily given in the same form to all men, but because all men are willing parties to an agreement to cut it up and think about it that way. Such an agreement is obligatory throughout a speech community and is codified in the patterns of the language. People in different cultures think differently, he said, because they are parties to different agreements.

When Whorf's hypothesis is pushed to the limit, it follows that translation between languages must be impossible. Indeed, many close students of the translation process have concluded that the perfect rendition of a literary or poetic work in another language probably is impossible. A good translator can give an approximate reformulation in a second language, but good translators are usually modest about their claims of perfection. And no one would claim that translation is a matter of making word-for-word substitutions; the first devices for mechanical translation worked that way, and the results were largely unintelligible.

The more different two societies are, the more difficult it is to translate from the language of one into the language of the other. Bilingual dictionaries can illustrate the point. An English-German dictionary is relatively simple, whereas it is difficult to compile an English-Zulu dictionary, because the cultures in which English and Zulu are spoken are so different. Monolingual speakers of English are largely ignorant of the cultural conventions on which Zulu is based, but the culture of German-speaking people is enough like the culture of English-speaking people so that many important conceptual distinctions can be taken for granted.

No one would expect the Eskimo to have a word for palm tree or the Zulu to have a word for snow. Nor would anyone expect the Eskimo or the Zulu to have words for esoteric concepts like "debenture" or "psycholinguistics." One would assume, however, that there is some core of lexical concepts so basic to human life that every language must have words for them. To a first approximation this assumption is correct, but it is surprising how short the list of universal concepts is—not more than 200 or 300 at most.

Chapter 3 discussed attempts to use lexical comparisons in order to estimate the times at which different languages diverged from a common parent language. Initially these studies used a list of 200 basic concepts, but after some experience trying to find words for all those concepts in a variety of exotic languages, the list was reduced to 100. Different languages carve the world up differently. Even for

One Hundred Universal Lexical Concepts

In order to compare the number of cognate words in historically related languages, the linguist Morris Swadesh constructed lists of concepts he judged to be so basic that every language would have words for them. His first list had 200 items, but many of them proved unsatisfactory when languages outside the Indo-European family were studied. The following list of 100 "diagnostic items" was then selected:

1.	I	26.	root	51.	breasts	76.	rain
2.	thou	27.	bark	52.	heart	77.	stone
3.	we	28.	skin	53.	liver	78.	sand
4.	this	29.	flesh	54.	drink	79.	earth
5.	that	30.	blood	55.	eat	80.	cloud
6.	who	31.	bone	56.	bite	81.	smoke
7.	what	32.	grease	57.	see	82.	fire
8.	not	33.	egg	58.	hear	83.	ash
9.	all	34.	horn	59.	know	84.	burn
10.	many	35.	tail	60.	sleep	85.	path
11.	one	36.	leather	61.	die	86.	mountain
12.	two	37.	hair	62.	kill	87.	red
13.	big	38.	head	63.	swim	88.	green
14.	long	39.	ear	64.	fly	89.	yellow
15.	small	40.	eye	65.	walk	90.	white
16.	woman	41.	nose	66.	come	91.	black
17.	man	42.	mouth	67.	lie	92.	night
18.	person	43.	tooth	68.	sit	93.	hot
19.	fish	44.	tongue	69.	stand	94.	cold
20.	bird	45.	claw	70.	give	95.	full
21.	dog	46.	foot	71.	say	96.	new
22.	louse	47.	knee	72.	sun	97.	good
23.	tree	48.	hand	73.	moon	98.	round
24.	seed	49.	belly	74.	star	99.	dry
25.	leaf	50.	neck	75.	water	100.	name

It is generally assumed that these concepts are expressed by words likely to be used in everyday speech, that the words are learned by children at an early age and that they are seldom borrowed by one language from another. With this list, Swadesh estimated that the rate of change in Indo-European languages was 14 percent per millennium.

something as universal as the parts of the body, it is difficult to find equivalent words in all languages. In English, for example, the word "eye" can refer either to the thing that opens and closes in the upper part of the face or to the eyeball; the Japanese word refers only to the facial feature, not to the eyeball; the Mongolian word refers only to the eyeball, not to the facial feature. Can these three words be taken as equivalent? In many languages the word used to refer to the foot refers to the whole leg, not merely to the part we call "foot." In Navaho one word is used for both "head" and human "hair," another is used for the hair of animals and so on. It is not always easy to find equivalent everyday words, even for this carefully selected list of concepts.

Eugene A. Nida of the American Bible Society is a linguist whose vast knowledge of lexical differences comes from experience in translating the Bible into many different languages. Nida gives an illuminating example of the importance of the cultural context. In one of the Motilone dialects of Colombia, the single word eto·kapa means to hatch out eggs, to commit suicide and to make corn cakes. For speakers of this language, three meanings that seem unrelated to us are thought of as three different ways of using the same word. In that society, a corpse is wrapped in a fetal position before burial, so a person who commits suicide is thought of as making himself into an egg-shaped object. And in making corn cakes, the corn is molded into egg-shaped lumps. Without a thorough knowledge of the Motilone culture, it would not be possible for us to deduce a single coherent concept from the English translations of the word eto·kapa.

Most people live their daily lives without encountering any of these translation problems, and therefore they seldom notice the cultural presuppositions underlying their own words. It is possible, however, to parallel Nida's example in reverse. Imagine the Indian's revenge. A Motilone visits England or the United States, studies the language and returns to Colombia with the following account: "In English the single word "newspaper" means both a sheaf of large sheets of paper with writing on them and a kind of commercial organization where people work. For speakers of this language, two meanings that seem unrelated to us are thought of as two different ways of using the same word. In that society, the sheaf of papers is manufactured by the people who work in the commercial organization. Without a thorough knowledge of their culture, it would not be possible for us to deduce a single coherent concept from its Motilone translations."

If the person from Colombia wished to enlarge on this example, it could be pointed out that we say "He is reading a newspaper" and "He works for a newspaper"; however, although we say "He is reading a book," we do not say "He works for a book" to mean that he works for a book publisher. We do not contrast two senses of "book" in the same way we contrast two meanings of "newspaper." This observation could lead to speculations about the cultural context: we may speak of newspapers and books differently because all issues of newspapers look alike and newspapers are published regularly, whereas books vary considerably in appearance and regularity of publication.

Note that this cultural background about the publishing business is not something a lexicographer would be likely to include in a dictionary of English or, for that matter, of French, German or Spanish, where the same double use of the word for newspaper is found. People who live in societies where these languages are spoken acquire such general knowledge in the course of participating in the cultural life of their societies. But the example illustrates the kind of question lexicographers constantly face: should the dictionary contain one or two definitions of "newspaper"? Are these two senses of "newspaper" as different as, say, the two senses of "port" meaning harbor and "port" meaning wine?

It will be helpful to distinguish two levels of meaning differences: alternative senses and extended senses. A word can have alternative senses, as "port" does; then each alternative sense can be used in extended senses, as it is when we extend "port" to include the container in which the wine is bottled. In these terms the question becomes, Are the two senses of "newspaper" alternative senses or is one of them an extended sense?

It is not an easy question to answer in any principled way,

but this kind of question comes up repeatedly in the compilation of dictionaries. In its most general form the question is, How ought we to distinguish between linguistic information that should go in the dictionary and general cultural information that should go in an encyclopedia? Somehow, lexicographers have to answer this question one way or another for every word in the dictionary.

A good desk dictionary is one of those modern conveniences we take for granted without stopping to realize how much information is packed into it, how much work was required to compile it or what the world would be like without it. The fact that we do have dictionaries, however, tempts us to think that lexical knowledge is distinct from general knowledge. Because lexicographers are able to draw a line, it is all too easy to assume that a person's lexical knowledge—the dictionary in a person's head—is also separated from everything else he knows.

When we raise the question of how lexical knowledge is organized in a person's memory, therefore, we must remember that a desk dictionary is just a desk dictionary, not a psychological theory about the structure of human memory. Although the dictionary in our head contains much of the information that is contained in a desk dictionary, our mental dictionary must be organized differently—it is not alphabetized in sequence; we can enter it two ways (with a word in search of a meaning or with a meaning in search of a word), and there is no sharp distinction between lexical information and general knowledge and belief.

As long as we keep these differences in mind, however, the structure of a dictionary entry can provide a useful guide to the kinds of information that must be associated with every word in a person's memory. What does the dictionary entry contain? A dictionary gives the pronunciation, the syntactic category and the meaning of each word. Large dictionaries usually contain some pragmatic information about usage and appropriate contexts of use. It seems reasonable to assume that all these kinds of information are also associated with each word in a person's mental lexicon. Let us consider each kind in turn.

First, phonological information. The sound of a word is

usually sufficient for us to gain access to (or to reconstruct, depending on your theory of memory) other information we have about that word. But we must also be able to go from meanings to the sounds that express them.

In speaking or writing we often feel there is a word we want but cannot think of—it is right on the tip of the tongue. This tantalizing feeling can be induced by reading dictionary meanings for infrequently used words and asking people to guess the words. When you hit a word they feel sure they know but cannot think of, you will find they can describe it: they can tell you the sound it starts or ends with or the number of syllables it has. If you tell them the word, they recognize immediately whether it is the one they were searching for. Thus, it is possible to obtain some psychological evidence about how words are organized phonologically in our memories.

Second, information about the syntactic category of a word must also be included in the mental lexicon. Chapter 8 introduced these categories as a necessary step in formulating syntactic rules, but they are more than convenient fictions of syntactic theory.

The most obvious evidence that lexical memory is organized with respect to syntactic categories is that people do not get the categories mixed up when they speak. They do not use verbs when articles are required or adverbs where nouns must go. We do not have to know what the categories are called in order to speak the language, but we must respect every word's privileges of occurrence.

This knowledge is fundamental to our ability to speak and understand a language. It is not surprising, therefore, that it can be elicited even in situations that do not involve full sentences—in word-association tests, for example: "Tell me the first word you think of when I say x," where x can be any word at all. Adults consistently reply with a word in the same syntactic category as the probe word x. If the probe word is the adjective "cold," for example, most adults will reply with the adjective "hot." Before about seven or eight years of age, however, children seldom do this, though we must suppose they "know" the categories in the sense that their speech conforms to them. Children are more likely to reply with a word that can be used in the same sentence with the probe word. Thus, given the adjective "cold," children are likely to reply with a noun like "snow."

Third, semantic information takes up most of the space in a dictionary; it probably takes up even more in our head. In a dictionary, a word is defined in terms of other words, and relatively little is said about conceptual relations between words or about general knowledge associated with the things words refer to. In the mental lexicon, some words must refer directly to things and events, and the network of conceptual relations between words is extensive and mixed inextricably with general and cultural knowledge.

Many weighty tomes have been written about semantics, because it is a deep and baffling subject. Unfortunately, after centuries of discussion by philosophers, linguists, psychologists and countless others, we still have no definition of "meaning" that is universally accepted.

For nominal terms, it seems reasonable to say that a person knows the meaning of a word if he can identify instances that the word refers to. We know the meaning of "gold," for example, if we can identify instances of it. But we are in trouble already! Many people talk about gold, but few can accurately identify instances of it. It takes a metallurgist to tell whether something really is gold. King Hiero asked Archimedes whether his crown was pure gold. Does that mean the king did not know what gold was because he could not identify an instance of it? Or does it mean that being able to identify instances is merely part of the meaning of a word? If it is merely part, what is the rest? And even if this theory of meaning worked for nominal terms, we would still need another theory for important words like "not," "ought," "good," "it" and "some," which are meaningful yet do not seem to refer to anything.

When we look at meaning relations between words, the situation is just as complex as it is for relations between words and things. For nominal terms, a hierarchic scheme seems to summarize a vast range of meaning relations between words: things named "husband" are included among the things named "man," men are included in people, people are animals, animals are objects. The words "husband" and "wife" are related in meaning because they both express many of the same concepts and differ only with respect to sex; the words "husband" and "tree," on the other hand, express fewer concepts in common and therefore are less closely related in meaning. Class inclusion, however, is only one of many meaning relations between words. When we try systematically to catalogue other relations, we find so many and so much diversity that we can only conclude that the contents of the lexicon are as untidy as the human mind it serves.

It is not that we cannot formulate and test many interesting generalizations about both reference and the relations between words. The problem is to fit those interesting parts together into something resembling a scientific theory.

Perhaps this sprawling heterogeneity is essential. Many artificial languages have been invented—logic, mathematics, musical notation, computer languages—that are much tidier and that, within their own limited domains, are more efficient than natural language. But only a natural language enables us to talk about anything and everything.

It is not merely that we can invent new names for anything. Naming is important, but it is not indispensable, because we do not need a special word for something in order to talk about it. The essential thing is that built into the core of every natural language are ways to represent all of the basic concepts we use to deal with ourselves and our world. There are ways to talk about life, people, space, time, quantity; ways to distinguish between shapes, colors, movements, possessions, kinfolk; ways to assert or deny; ways to distinguish the possible from the actual; ways to relate what is novel to what is familiar; ways to identify cause and effect; ways to express beliefs, desires, emotions; ways to distinguish the particular from the general; ways to summarize or expand, persuade or dissuade, inform or deceive, pray or curse—the list goes on and on. If natural languages are not adequate to express everything, at least they are adequate to express whatever we might think about anything.

To achieve this versatility, a human language must have a corresponding variety of lexical resources to draw on. But consider what this costs in memory capacity. For each entry

Word Probabilities

Although some people have larger vocabularies than others have, a few words are used so frequently that everybody knows them. The 50 most frequent words in speech make up 60 percent of what we say ("I" ranks first); the 50 most frequent in writing make up 45 percent of what we write ("the" ranks first). Most overworked words are monosyllables. The commonest verbs and nouns are among the first learned by children, have many different senses and (if word length is held constant) are the easiest to say, read, remember or think of.

If word frequencies are tabulated and the words ranked from most frequent to least frequent, a simple formula describes the relation. This relation is known as Zipf's law, after the linguist George Kingsley Zipf.

If p_r is the probability of the rth most frequent word, then

$$p_r = \frac{0.1}{r}.$$

When plotted on log-log coordinates, this function gives a straight line with a slope of -1.

Zipf showed that the formula gives a good approximation of word probabilities in many languages (if "word" is defined as any sequence of successive letters bounded by spaces).

Zipf's law was once thought to reflect some deep psychobiological principle peculiar to the human mind. It was proposed, for example, that if we intercepted signals from outer space, we would know they came from intelligent beings if we could fit them to Zipf's law. It has since been proved, however, that completely random processes can also show this statistical regularity.

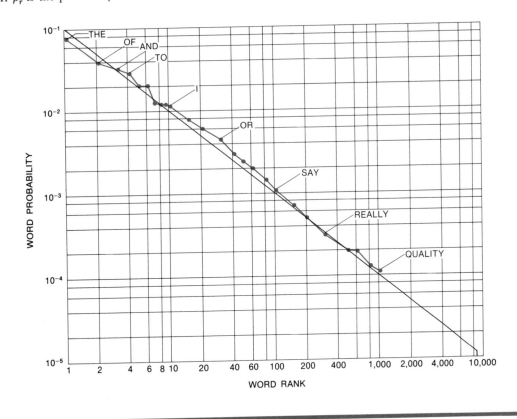

a person must store phonological, syntactic and heterogeneous semantic and pragmatic information that must be rich enough to express his general knowledge. And there are on the order of 100,000 such entries. The mental lexicon represents an enormous investment of memory.

Neurologists have called certain areas of the cortex of the brain "association areas," not because they know associations are made there but because those areas do not receive sensory input or send out motor commands. Association areas are small in monkeys, get bigger in apes and are very large in man. Students of the evolution of the human brain generally assume that its increase in size did not arise from enlargement of the sensory or motor areas but from the growth of association areas separating and interrelating the sensory and motor areas—from what is called growth by intercalation.

There is an analogy here with modern computers. It has been found that the size of a computer memory can be expanded relatively easily without any basic redesign of the processing unit that uses the memory. The analogy suggests that much of the growth in the size of the human brain was an expansion of the neural tissue available for memory.

Why did larger memories suddenly become so valuable for survival? Presumably, because there was suddenly something worth remembering. What could that have been? We can never know for sure, but clearly the information in our mental lexicon—not to mention our mental encyclopedia—could not be stored in anything less than a prodigious memory. Perhaps symbolic communication came first, then the large brain followed because it enhanced the selective advantage of those who could communicate symbolically.

Some scientists believe human language is what it is because it reflects the way our brain works; others believe our brain works the way it does because language has shaped it so. I believe that both are right. Human brains and human language have shaped each other. Children must be born with brains capable of learning language, and language must be the kind of thing that children's brains can learn. To ask which is cause and which effect is like asking whether running is the result of the action of the right leg or the left.

10

The Acquisition of Language

A three-week-old infant, propped up in a tilted basket, is sucking on a nipple, head motionless and eyes riveted on a colorful picture straight ahead. A loudspeaker emits [ba] at regular intervals: [ba], [ba], [ba]. The sound changes to [pa], and the infant's sucking rate increases abruptly. As the loudspeaker goes on saying [pa], [pa], [pa], the sucking gradually slows.

The nipple does not give nutriment. It contains a pressure-sensitive device for recording the rate of sucking. When infants are interested, their sucking rate increases; as they get bored, it decreases. These facts are the basis for a technique for studying infants' ability to discriminate speech sounds.

One of the first studies with this technique used synthetic stop consonants and varied the voice onset time in small steps through the range that, in adult speech, differentiates [b] from [p]. If the change did not cross the category boundary, infants did not notice it; when it did cross the boundary, however, their sucking rate increased abruptly. Subsequent studies with [ba] and [ga] showed similar categorical discrimination; neither children nor adults discriminated the transitional chirps made by the isolated transition into the second formant (see page 68). In short, infants seem to respond to these sounds much as adults do.

Infants one or two months old could not have learned these discriminations. The boldest explanation is also the simplest: human infants are born with feature detectors sensitive to certain distinctive acoustic features of human speech. The human auditory system does not merely develop a special mode of perception for speech, the basis for that special mode is innate. Some workers began to question this explanation, however, when it was subsequently shown that similar results for voice onset times can be obtained with chinchillas, which are not noted for their use of vocal communication. Perhaps our articulatory system evolved to take advantage of perceptual mechanisms far older than speech in mammalian evolution.

How the results with chinchillas should be interpreted is not entirely clear, and further animal experiments using various speech cues are being conducted. The status of innate feature detectors for speech cues is, therefore, still under debate. Why research should be directed toward finding innate abilities to process language, however, is reasonably clear.

The discovery of language during the childhood of every individual is one of the wonders of human life. Learning a language is a lot of work, even for someone who already knows what languages are; babies have no language in which to understand explanations. Anyway, parents are not able to explain language—they know how to use language, not how to explain it. An infant must pick it up as an apprentice, through participation in the social game of language. Part of the wonder is that the apprenticeship is taken up with such enthusiasm; there must be some innate predisposition to be interested in communication.

The strength of this need to communicate is illustrated most poignantly by congenitally deaf children who are not exposed to sign language. A parent's motives for preventing signing are good; oral education enables the children to become members of the larger social community. But learning to speak without acoustic feedback is a difficult, slow process; the urge to communicate cannot wait. Deaf children in schools for oral education have been observed to gesture to one another spontaneously behind the teacher's back. One careful study of six deaf children who had not entered (or had only begun) school and had not been exposed to any standard sign language showed that they spontaneously invented structured systems of signs with simple phrase-structure grammars. It is remarkable that it is possible for chimpanzees to learn such systems; it is even more remarkable that it is impossible to prevent human children from doing so.

Even for a hearing child, however, the task is not simple. Good parents try to help. They name things and reward the most approximate imitations. There is a special dialect, often called motherese, that shortens sentences and simplifies syntax. It has not been proved that these tactics are really helpful; certainly they are not necessary. What is necessary is that someone be willing to play the language game with the child. Whatever a child's innate predispositions, he cannot acquire his native tongue without a chance to practice it.

Many universal features of human languages seem both complex and arbitrary. With a little language engineering it would not be difficult to devise simpler systems of vocal communication, systems that should be easier for children to learn (and for linguists to explain). But that misses the point. Even if such a rationalized language were developed and successfully imposed on all living adults, within one generation things would be back to their present state. We are not considering a teaching situation where the master sets arbitrary problems for the pupil. We are considering a social situation where master and apprentice interact; their interaction depends as much on the apprentice's contribution as on the master's. The adult's language has the features it does precisely because those are features young children find most natural and easy to learn.

The problem, therefore, is not to understand how a child acquires language in spite of its complexities but rather to understand how the complexities of adult language are shaped by innate predispositions of the child. Viewed in these terms, searching for the child's innate abilities to process language is an obvious strategy for research.

Normal children the world over pass through a series of similar stages on their way to becoming fluent speakers of their native tongue. Given normal social support, the acquisition of language proceeds in a regular sequence; some children pass through more rapidly than others, but the sequence seems invariant. If all children lived in a world that offered them language in the same order, unfolding progressively the way a good textbook is written, the regularity of development could be explained in terms of regularity of experience. Most students of child language, however, find it more plausible to attribute this regularity not to uniform experience but to the regularity of biological processes of maturation. What a child learns will depend on opportunity; how it is learned depends more on the child.

Some evidence concerning biological aspects of language acquisition comes from the development of hemispheric specialization. In most adults, language functions are controlled by the left hemisphere of the brain. The right hemisphere can perform these functions, however; if there is some early damage to the left, the normal picture may be reversed. Lateralization may be innate, but its signs appear gradually in children; not until four or five years of age are there unmistakable signs that it is occurring.

There is an interesting question here. According to one view the left hemisphere has a small initial advantage over the right—it develops slightly faster. When speech begins, and the control of midline articulatory structures from a single hemisphere becomes important, the left hemisphere is better prepared to take over this control. Once speech is lateralized, the cognitive processes involved in hearing and comprehending speech naturally follow. By the time precise manipulospatial skills develop, around the age of six or seven, the left hemisphere has already been heavily preempted for language, and these functions come to be controlled predominantly by the right hemisphere. In the normal course of development, therefore, both hemispheres have become specialized by the age of 10 or 11. Thereafter, injury to the left hemisphere can result in permanent disabilities of speech or language, because the right hemisphere is no longer able to take over these functions.

The innate predispositions that enable children to learn language, therefore, may not be genetically specialized in the left hemisphere. According to this theory the hemispheric specialization seen in most adults is not genetically preformed but arises from interactions between the genetic endowment and the conditions under which development occurs.

Critics of this view do not believe that the two hemispheres are equally capable of learning language. Children in whom one hemisphere must be surgically removed during the first year of life can learn to talk. Careful analysis of their speech, however, indicates that children who retain only their left hemisphere develop a more complicated and more nearly normal pattern of speech than do children who retain only their right hemisphere. Such children may not be representative of the normal population, but these observations by Dr. Maureen Dennis at the Hospital for Sick Children in Toronto strongly suggest that the left hemisphere of the human brain does inherit some special organization that prepares it to take control of language functions.

This disagreement may take years of research to settle. In either view—whether or not the two hemispheres are equally capable of acquiring language—however, the universal regularities that are seen in the development of child language are not dependent on any single neural structure. Presumably, they arise from a much more abstract capacity of the human nervous system to learn language. After many centuries of debate about the relative importance of heredity versus learning in human development, it is sobering to realize that a major contribution of heredity may be the innate ability for particular kinds of learning.

What are the universal regularities in the development of language? A brief survey, illustrated by examples taken from studies of English-speaking children, may be helpful.

Children's first words are tied to gestures. Perhaps the first gesture children understand is direction of gaze: they look in the direction their mother is looking. Long before they have words they will spontaneously pick things up and show them to adults. Pointing with the eyes leads to pointing with the arm; pointing then differentiates into a "look at" gesture and a more insistent "give me" gesture that adds grasping movements (and sometimes whining) to the basic directional sign. These gestures perform the same acts of asserting and requesting that are later performed with language and are naturally thought of as precursors to language.

When the first words appear, between the ages of 10 and 15 months, these gestures accompany them; vocalization is used more to attract attention than to communicate information. "Dada" may be uttered while looking at father; "mama," accompanied by whining and the "give me" gesture, may be uttered for any desired object. In short, communicative competence begins to develop before linguistic competence.

Vocalizations also change and develop during the first year, but more in the spirit of play than of communication. Presumably, babbling and other vocal play provide an opportunity to correlate vocal maneuvers with their acoustic consequences. The shape of the infant's vocal tract is changing; as the throat cavity grows in size, the variety of vowels increases and so does the variety of consonants. During the first year a child will produce a far greater variety of sounds than will be needed in adult speech, sounds that could not result from imitation. Moreover, the early babbling includes sounds like [l] and [r] that the child will need later but is apparently unable to produce voluntarily until he is much older.

During the first year these two streams—communication and vocalization—flow in separate channels. During the second year they come together as the child learns to coordinate vocalization in the service of communication, and true language begins to develop.

Almost immediately a third stream joins the first two. As the child becomes able to utter different words while gesturing in different ways, cognitive accomplishments make themselves manifest. From early experience, children learn that objects are enduring entities that differ in how they look, taste, feel and respond to manipulation. These first conceptual distinctions motivate the first communicative distinctions. The earliest words children use fall into two major types: names for concrete objects ("ball," "cookie") and words used in social interactions ("more," "bye-bye"). The objects named, moreover, are manipulable objects like food, toys and body parts; children do not name things, however obvious or important, that just sit there: walls, tables, trees, grass. Children's first concepts develop from

Child Language

The following conversation between two four-year-old children was recorded in a playroom situation:

GIRL: [*on toy telephone*] David!
BOY: [*not picking up second phone*] I'm not home.
GIRL: When you'll be back?
BOY: I'm not here already.
GIRL: But *when you'll be back?*
BOY: Don't you know if I'm gone already, I went *before* so I can't talk to you!

sensorimotor interactions, and those concepts are apparent in their first words. Children talk about what they know.

These first, single-word utterances serve a variety of functions for a child. Some theorists consider them to be one-word sentences; others deny that children have any conception of sentences at this age. Parents feel they can tell when "dada" should be expanded into "There is daddy" and when it should be expanded into "I want daddy to come here," and relatively objective psychologists often agree. But whether these expanded sentential concepts should be attributed to the child is not an easy question to answer.

When children start to combine words, methods of syntactic analysis can be brought to bear. Two-word utterances begin to appear at about 15 to 18 months, usually with a slight pause between them, then with more fluency. Thereafter, the steady increase in average sentence length is the most reliable yardstick for the child's growth in linguistic competence. The complications of structure that they learn almost all add to the length of their sentences.

It is probably grammatical complexity, however, not the sheer number of words, that limits what a child can do. For example, interrogative sentences are not much longer than the corresponding declaratives, but it takes children a long time to get them right. Aux Inversion seems especially difficult. The first step in learning to ask questions may actually be correct: the child may ask "What's this?" But then "what's" is analyzed into two words and the question becomes "This is what?" by analogy with "This is daddy's book." The next step shows mastery of Wh-Fronting, and questions like "What this is?" are heard. Thousands of such questions may be asked over a period of two or three years before the auxiliary verb is moved in front of the subject: "What is this?" (in this sentence the auxiliary verb is used as a main verb). Aux Inversion is first mastered in yes-no questions like "Is this daddy's book?" and only later extended to Wh-questions. When it is extended, it is used with some Wh-words before others. The child knows the transformational rule, but it may take months to discover all the Wh-words that trigger this rule. The progression of interrogative forms the child uses, however, can only be explained in terms of the successive mastery of transformational rules.

One construction in English that has proved diagnostic of a child's syntactic knowledge is the tag question. Tag questions are requests for confirmation: "John will come, won't he?" or "You won't do it, will you?" The form of the tag varies with the form of the sentence it is tagged to. If the sentence is affirmative, the tag is negative; if the sentence is negative, the tag is affirmative. The tag itself is short, two or three words long, but its syntactic relation to the preceding sentence is relatively complex.

Consider how "won't he" is derived from "John will come." The subject of the sentence is pronominalized, giving "he will come." Then it is negated, giving "he will not come." Next the negative is contracted, giving "he won't come." Then Aux Inversion makes it a question: "won't he come?" Finally, deletion of the rest of the verb phrase yields "won't he?" All in all, tag questions give the grammatical rules a good workout. Children do not produce this kind of tag question until they are about five years old— not, that is, until they have already demonstrated their mastery of all the components in other, simpler sentence constructions.

It is often said that children acquire their language in large measure through learning by imitation. In some general sense this claim must be true, because children do end up talking like their parents. The usual sense of "imitation," however, is immediate echoing of what was just heard. In this sense, children do not imitate the speech of adults, even when we ask them to. If the sentence to be imitated contains words or constructions the child has not mastered, they will be omitted in the imitation.

In one study, a child 29 months old was heard to say, "If you finish your eggs all up, Daddy, you can have your coffee." When asked to imitate this sentence immediately, she said, "After you finish your eggs all up then you can have your coffee, Daddy." Ten minutes later, when she had become interested in other things, she was again given her own sentence to imitate; she could say only, "You can have coffee, Daddy, after." One reason children do not imitate

---

Why Do Children Learn?

What impels the child to "improve" his speech at all remains something of a mystery. We can take "improve" simply to mean "bring into closer approximation to the speech of older persons around the child." It is surprising that there should be any mystery about the forces impelling improvement because it is just this aspect of the process that most people imagine that they understand. Surely the improvement is a response to selection pressures of various kinds; ill-formed or incomplete utterances must be less effective than well-formed and complete utterances in accomplishing the child's intent; parents probably approve of well-formed utterances and disapprove or correct the ill-formed. These ideas sound sensible and may be correct but the still scant evidence available does not support them. . . .

In general the parents seemed to pay no attention to bad syntax nor did they even seem to be aware of it. They approved or disapproved an utterance usually on the grounds of the truth value of the proposition which the parents supposed the child intended to assert. This is a surprising outcome to most middle-class parents, since they are generally under the impression that they correct the child's speech. From inquiry and observation I find that what parents correct is pronunciation, "naughty" words, and regularized irregular allomorphs like *digged* or *goed*. These facts of the child's speech seem to penetrate parental awareness. But syntax—the child saying, for instance, 'Why the dog won't eat?' instead of 'Why won't the dog eat?' seems to be automatically set right in the parent's mind, with the mistake never registering as such.

In sum, then, we do not presently have evidence that there are selection pressures of any kind operating on children to impel them to bring their speech into line with adult models. . . . A radically different possibility is that children work out rules for the speech they hear, passing from levels of lesser to greater complexity, simply because the human species is programmed at a certain period in its life to operate in this fashion on linguistic input.

ROGER BROWN
A First Language: The Early Stages

well is that they are not often asked to imitate sentences that express their own communicative intentions at the moment. Or, putting it the other way round, because the sentences that are available to imitate do not often express their own communicative intentions, imitation is not a useful way for children to learn to talk.

It is difficult to explain questions like "What this is?" on the basis of imitation. Further evidence for some process more active than imitation comes from errors children make consistently, although they do not hear their parents say them. For example, a young child may for a short period have both the present tense "throw" and the past tense "threw" in his vocabulary. Then from experience with regular verbs the child induces the rule that past-tense verbs are formed by adding "-ed" and so begins adding "-ed" to all verbs. This rule works well for regular verbs, but it is wrong for irregular verbs—for example, "throwed." This overgeneralization of the morphological rule persists for a long time; it is not infrequently heard in kindergartens and even in first-grade classrooms. Similar overgeneralizations occur with irregular plurals: "foots" instead of "feet" is common. When children say "runned" and "tooths" they are not imitating their parents.

Conscientious parents usually correct such errors in word formation, but they seldom correct interrogatives like "What this is?" Because these ill-formed questions are perfectly intelligible and are accepted without correction by adults, it is puzzling to understand why children stop saying "What this is?" and start saying "What is this?" If they simply persisted, in just a generation or two they could win the battle—Aux Inversion would no longer follow Wh-Fronting even in adult language. There is no indication, however, that this simplification of English grammar (if it really is a simplification) is likely to occur. Interrogatives like "What this is?" appear in a child's speech without imitation, and they disappear without correction (without contingent rewards or punishments).

Apparently the kind of rule learning that is characteristic of language differs from the learning processes that have been studied so extensively in thousands of psychological experiments. The capacity for this kind of rule learning may be unique to language and specific to *Homo sapiens.*

Although children's rapid mastery of syntax between 18 and 60 months of age has attracted much attention and inspired many studies of child language, their rapid mastery of the lexicon is no less impressive. Vocabulary tests given to children lead to the estimate that a six-year-old child of average i.q. is learning new words at a rate of about 22 per day (or about 14 root words per day). Nobody teaches them 22 words a day. Their minds are like little vacuum pumps designed by nature to suck up words. Children learn words spontaneously while playing the language game. We are only beginning to develop methods for studying how they do it.

It is impossible to talk about the acquisition of language without talking separately about its various aspects—about the development of phonology, about the mastery of morphological or syntactic rules, about cognitive development and the growth of vocabulary, about social skills for using language in an increasing variety of ways. One cannot study a child very long, however, without recognizing that all these aspects are organically integrated and mutually interdependent. How sound, meaning and use work together in a developing whole is a major source of wonder. Although we see it happening around us every day, we are years away from really understanding it.

Meanwhile, it is fun to speculate.

Ernst Heinrich Haeckel was the first German biologist who wholeheartedly endorsed Charles Darwin's theory of evolution. It was in enthusiastic support of evolutionary theory that, in 1866 he proposed his "fundamental biogenetic law": ontogeny recapitulates phylogeny (individual development repeats the evolution of the species). The human embryo begins as a unicellular organism and passes rapidly through a developmental sequence that recapitulates our human ancestry: fish, amphibian, mammal, human. Because there may be only a few ways to transform a single cell into an adult human being, the suggestion that the developmental way is similar to the evolutionary way has always had its adherents.

Most biologists long ago rejected the claim that this might be a serious scientific law. The similarities Haeckel observed are interesting, but they provide no useful evidence about human evolution. Today it seems to be widely agreed that under no circumstances can a description of ontogenetic development be taken as evidence for phylogenetic evolution.

Any suggestion that human language might have evolved through the same stages that characterize the development of language in children must, therefore, be recognized as pure speculation. With direct evidence about the origin of language as scarce as it is, however, Haeckel's speculation seems little worse than any other. And some consider child language the best indirect evidence we have about primitive communication.

Consider it. There is, first of all, the matter of the high larynx. It serves to prevent babies from choking before they learn to coordinate their alimentary and respiratory tracts. But as the larynx descends into the neck we can observe a progressive enrichment in the child's phonetic repertoire— perhaps there is a clue here to what early speech sounded like.

At birth a child utters sounds reflexly to express emotions, much as living primates do. Shortly thereafter we see the appearance of gestural communication, under voluntary control. Then gestures are accompanied by spoken names for objects pointed to or reached for; the names become progressively differentiated and become independent of the gestural system. These words are soon combined, though with little respect for word order. As utterances grow longer, recognizable syntactic patterns are adopted to organize them. Learning the inflated vocabulary of modern industrial society continues into adulthood—if, indeed, it ever stops.

Once we get over a distaste for looking at children as living fossils at different stages of evolution, the above description of their language development does not seem an unreasonable scenario for the evolution of human language.

11

Conversation

Any complex subject can be approached in different ways, at different levels of abstraction. There are usually structural aspects to be described; in the case of human language, this approach leads to theories of grammar and syntax. There are usually processes to be carried out; in the case of language, the consideration of process leads to psychological theories of speech perception, language acquisition and memory for linguistic messages. There are often larger ends achieved as a consequence of performing those processes; in the case of language, this approach leads to pragmatic theories of language use in social contexts.

At the beginning of chapter 7, these three approaches were presented as alternative definitions of language, as alternative answers to the question, What is language? We have now explored some of the insights that follow from definitions in terms of structure and process. It remains for us to consider what language is in terms of our social conventions for using it. To illustrate this approach, let us look next at that important and ubiquitous form of social interaction we call conversation.

Perhaps the most obvious thing to say about conversation is that it is a cooperative interaction: participants must agree on a topic, they must take turns developing it and their contributions must be intelligible, relevant and truthful. Our human disposition to participate in such interactions is no trivial thing to be taken for granted. Just as human evolution provided biological bases underlying and shaping linguistic structures and processes, so it also pro-

121

vided a biological basis for this kind of cooperative social behavior.

It was once believed that primates are held together in troops primarily by the bond of sex, because reproduction can occur at any time during the year. It is now known, however, that some monkeys confine breeding to a well-marked season, yet live in troops throughout the year. Primates are profoundly social, with or without sexual relations. Indeed, in those monkeys who do have special breeding seasons, sex seems to be a disruptive factor: fighting increases between the males, not because they are denied access to a female but simply because they are more aggressive and difficult to live with. The social group is maintained not because of sex but in spite of it.

Social relations in primate groups are complex. The troop is usually dominated by one mature male or by a few mature males, and each member knows its place in the hierarchy. But there are bonds of affection between individuals, and sometimes in chimpanzees the dominance hierarchy is backed up by alliances among males. The dominance order seems to be a way of reducing the disruptive effects of fighting. And with fighting under control, other forms of social interaction can develop. Probably the most important is the bond between mother and infant, which often persists into adulthood and provides a focus for other social groupings within the troop.

Although the social life of monkeys and apes is rich, complex and adaptive, it is not characteristically cooperative. The beginnings of cooperation can be seen between mother and offspring, but there is nothing like the instinctive cooperation observed among the social insects. Laboratory experiments have shown that chimpanzees are able to cooperate in solving problems, but they seldom do so without special training. Somewhere in the evolution of human society the male was drawn into the mother-infant unit, lasting bonds were created between males and females and the way was opened for the family instead of the troop. The basic organization of a family unit must be cooperative.

Once the erect posture of early hominids freed their hands for carrying, it was possible for them to establish a home base, to gather or hunt food at some distance and to carry it back and share it with the whole group. Food sharing and the dividing of labor between paired males and females are characteristic of all primitive societies that exist today. Among hunters and gatherers, prestige goes to the one who is most generous, the one who does the most to provide for the others. Subhuman societies are characterized by competition and organized by dominance, whereas primitive human societies are characterized by cooperation and organized by kinship.

Cooperative problem solving is possible in the absence of language, but a way of life that depended on cooperative problem solving must have created a selective advantage for those best able to communicate effectively. Without language, communication is almost necessarily limited to the immediate present, here and now. With language, communication can be unhooked from the immediate context—we can speak of things there and then, thus vastly increasing our powers for anticipation, abstraction and deceit. Language provided an intellectual tool whose applications and implications we are still discovering.

Even when the topic is abstract or remote, however, most language is still used in face-to-face situations: a few people, alternating as speaker and hearers, talking about something of mutual interest. Whether for work or pleasure, everyone spends time sharing in conversational interactions.

What a group will talk about depends on their reasons for getting together, but we can tell a lot about what is going on even if we cannot understand the language they are using. We can tell who has power by observing who talks the most. We can tell whom a person likes by observing the one he or she talks to most. In a task-oriented group, we can tell who is resisting the work by observing who jokes and laughs the most. Indeed, social psychologists have found that we can tell a lot about people's personalities simply by watching them interact conversationally in small groups.

Conversations have certain characteristics that set them off from other forms of social interaction. Everybody has a chance to speak, but only one person speaks at a time; gaps between speakers are usually short; the order of speakers and

Communication Nets

In a conversational group, each person can send messages to and receive messages from any other member. In radio broadcasting, one person sends the same message to many others, who cannot reply. In a business organization, people can use telephones to communicate in pairs. Each of these situations illustrates a different communication net.

If a group has a problem that can only be solved by the cooperation of every member, the communication net that connects them will influence the way they proceed and the satisfaction they get from participation. For example, in experiments with five-person groups arranged either in a circle or in a wheel, it was found that the circle was unorganized, unstable, passed many more messages and was leaderless but satisfying to its members; the wheel was organized, stable, passed fewer messages and had a clearly recognized leader (the hub of the wheel) but did not satisfy four of the five members. Both groups, however, required about the same amount of time to solve the problem.

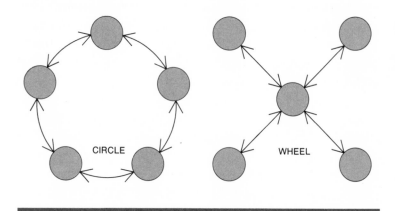

CIRCLE   WHEEL

the lengths of their speeches are not fixed in advance. In order to achieve this kind of interaction, participants must observe an ordered set of social conventions for taking turns. Highest priority is assigned to the convention that the next turn goes to the person addressed by the current speaker. If the current speaker does not indicate who is to take the next turn, the second convention is that it goes to whoever speaks first. And if no one speaks first, the third convention is that the current speaker can speak again.

The current speaker has a variety of ways to select the

next speaker, all based on conventions for pairs of linked utterances. Speakers can indicate whom they are talking to by naming them (or by looking at them or even by talking about something that only the addressee knows about); then they use a sentence that demands a direct response.

Detailed analysis of transcribed conversations shows a great variety of such linked pairs of adjacent utterances. For example, if the speaker asks a question of someone, the next turn should consist of that person giving an answer. If the speaker makes an offer or gives a compliment to someone, the next turn should accept or reject it. If the speaker makes a request of someone, the next turn should be responsive to the request. And so on.

There are also conventional ways to open conversations and more complicated conventions for closing them or changing the subject.

Young children have to learn these conventions. They frequently fail to elicit responses from adults, because they make assertions instead of using the first member of a linked pair of turns; they may abuse the question-answer convention by repeatedly asking "Why?"; they typically close a conversation by simply walking away.

The effect of these conversational conventions is to make much of what we say to each other highly dependent on the immediately antecedent context. If, for example, we want to say "The boy is reading a book," we must first set up an appropriate context:

A: Incidentally, Bill. Remember the boy you asked about?

B: Yeah.

A: Well, he's here in the library.

B: No kidding.

A: Yeah. He's reading a book.

"Incidentally" is a conventional signal for introducing a new topic. "Bill" designates the next speaker. "Remember the boy you asked about?" introduces the topic and demands an answer; sentences opening a new topic usually indicate why the speaker thinks the hearer should be interested in it. "Yeah" is the linked response; it acknowledges the topic and returns the initiative to A. With the topic established, "He's here in the library" substitutes the anaphoric pronoun "he" for the antecedent "the boy you asked about" and, because the phrase is not the first member of a linked pair of conversational turns, leaves B free to comment on the topic. "No kidding" acknowledges the assertion; it is a conventional signal for the preceding speaker to continue. "Yeah" does not mean "Yes, I am kidding" but signals compliance with the request to continue. Finally the groundwork is laid, and A can say "He's reading a book," which is almost (but not exactly) the sentence we wanted to say.

The substitution of the pronoun "he" for the antecedent definite noun phrase "the boy" is an example of anaphora, an important and pervasive linguistic phenomenon. To understand who "he" is, a hearer must be able to link the pronoun to its antecedent. Not only are there links between successive speakers, there must also be links between successive speeches. Language provides ways to signal the relation of the present sentence to its context—either to the preceding discourse or to the situation in which the sentence is used or to both. In particular, it provides a way to signal whether the sentence is about something already introduced or is introducing something new.

In English, we typically signal the first introduction of something by using the indefinite article "a." When we say the boy is reading "a book," it signals that this is the first time the book has been mentioned. Once introduced, it provides an antecedent for definite reference: "the book" or "it." When A opens with "Remember the boy you asked about?" he can use "the boy" because the boy has already been introduced in previous conversation. If A were to continue on his second turn by saying "Well, a boy's here in the library," the indefinite article would signal a different boy and A would owe B an explanation of how this second boy was relevant to the topic. A's use of the definite "he" in his second turn signals that A is still talking about the same boy.

Our deployment of pronouns is clearly governed by rules. We might ask, therefore, whether they are syntactic rules. For example, the sentence "After John ate, John fell asleep" strongly suggests that there are two Johns; if the speaker had been talking about a single John, he would have said "After John ate, he fell asleep," where the definite pronoun "he" clearly signals that it is the same John. On the basis of such observations, some linguists proposed that there must be a transformational rule that substitutes "he" for the second occurrence of "John" in such sentences.

Formulating a transformational rule that would specify when a pronoun and an antecedent noun phrase must corefer turned out to be difficult, because coreference is a semantic relation, not a syntactic relation. The next step, therefore, was to try to formulate an interpretive rule (rather than a syntactic rule) that would specify when pronoun and antecedent noun phrase must corefer. The problem with this approach was that "John" and "he" do not necessarily corefer in "After John ate, he fell asleep"; "he" could be an anaphor for someone else introduced previously. Instead of specifying when two noun phrases must corefer, therefore, the rule had to be stated in a way that specifies when they cannot corefer. It specifies, for example, that "he" and "John" cannot corefer in "He fell asleep after John ate."

The details of the rule are irrelevant here. The point is that our deployment of pronouns is not governed by syntactic rules and that all a semantic rule can say is what certain pronouns cannot refer to. Consider where this leaves the problem of deciding what an anaphoric pronoun does refer to. Apparently there must be still another level of rules governing our use of pronouns.

Take another example. In the sentence "John won the race from Bill because he had a good coach," we understand that "he" refers to John, whereas in "John won the race from Bill because he had a poor coach," we understand that "he" refers to Bill. We understand the sentences this way, not on the basis of linguistic rules but on the basis of our nonlinguistic knowledge that athletes with good coaches usually perform better than athletes with poor coaches.

We could be wrong, however. It is not senseless to say "John won the race from Bill because John had a poor coach." It might be an ironic way to express a low opinion of coaches. When we hear "John won the race from Bill because he had a poor coach," how do we decide whether the speaker expected us to draw the commonsense conclusion or to recognize that he was being ironic?

In short, we must make a judgment of the speaker's intention. What function did the speaker intend this sentence to serve? Given this judgment, we can then decide what "he" refers to. At this point we clearly need a functional theory of language use. Constructing this theory will not be easy. At present we are still trying to catalogue the questions such a theory should answer.

A central problem seems to be that most sentences are ambiguous out of context—they can mean different things in different contexts of use. Pronouns provide the most obvious illustration. "I was there" means very different things according to who says it. But "was" and "there" also pose problems of interpretation. Even for a given speaker, the sentence might be false at one time and true at some subsequent time; its meaning depends on the time it is uttered. And even for a given speaker at a given time, "there" can refer to many different places.

Sentences like "I was there" can be interpreted only in their context of use. Sentences that cannot be judged true or false out of context are called deictic sentences. "I was there" involves three kinds of deixis: "I" illustrates deixis of person, "was" illustrates deixis of time and "there" illustrates deixis of place. A pragmatic theory should explain how we are able to assign interpretations to such sentences in particular contexts of use. How, for example, "he" can be interpreted as "the boy B asked about" in the particular conversational context already described. A semantic theory should then explain how we decide whether the interpreted sentence is true or false.

Consider a different kind of problem. If a speaker says "John drinks," deixis poses no difficulties. But there is considerable difficulty in deciding, out of context, why he said it. Is he using the sentence to make an assertion, issue a warning, pronounce a judgment or suggest a source of refreshment? In other words, what kind of speech act does he want "John drinks" to count as on this particular occasion of its use?

According to one view, a pragmatic theory should not

only explain how we determine what proposition the sentence is being used to express in the given context but should also explain how we determine what speech act the sentence is being used to perform in that context. That is to say, the theory should specify the conditions that must obtain if the sentence is to count as a performance of a given speech act.

You borrow some money from a friend and say "I promise to pay it back Monday." To perform the act of promising, you must be able to pay the money and your friend must want you to pay it; it is not something you were going to do anyhow, and you must speak the promise so your friend can understand you. The critical thing is that you must accept a personal commitment to carry it out. These conditions are presupposed by the act. The presuppositions for issuing a

Deixis

Deixis" comes from a Greek word that means pointing or indicating. The earliest extant treatise on Greek grammar was written by Dionysus Thrax around 100 B.C. In it he dealt with the eight parts of speech recognized by his teacher, Aristarchus, which today we call noun, verb, pronoun, adverb, participle, article, conjunction and preposition. One kind of article he discussed was "deiktikos," which Roman grammarians translated as "demonstrativus" and English grammarians translated as "demonstrative." In English we classify demonstratives (this, that, these, those) as pronouns, not articles (the, a, an), but in early Greek there was no basis for distinguishing them.

The Greek word was revived in 1934 by the German psychologist Karl Bühler, who wanted a general term to refer to all the lexical and grammatical devices used to relate utterances to the spatio-temporal situations in which they are used. For example, in "I am here," "I" indicates the speaker and "here" indicates the speaker's location. The tense of a verb is also deictic: it indicates a time relative to (before, during or after) the time of the speaker's utterance.

The reference of nondeictic words like "cow" or "table" is generally considered to be part of their meaning. In contrast, deictic words have no fixed reference. They can be used even when the speaker doesn't know what he or she is referring to: people who are lost can always truthfully say "I am here," even though they do not know what place "here" refers to. The meaning of a deictic term must be stated as a rule for determining what the speaker is demonstrating by its use.

warning that you will do something are very similar to those for promising, except that it must be something your hearer does not want you to do.

Sentences beginning "I" and followed by present tense verbs like "promise," "warn," "ask," "congratulate," "christen," "order" and many others (sometimes with "hereby" before the verb) are called performatives. The act they are intended to perform is explicitly indicated in the act of performing it. However, you could have performed the same act by telling your friend, "You'll get it back Monday." In both sentences you would have had the same intention. Thus the sentences would have the same illocutionary force, to use the technical term invented by the Oxford philosopher J. L. Austin. In a different context, however, "You'll get it back Monday" could have the illocutionary force of an assertion, prediction or warning. In order to determine the speaker's intention, a hearer must decide from the context of use whether the presuppositions are met for promising, asserting, predicting or warning.

What happens when the presuppositions of a speech act are violated? For example, "Have you stopped beating your wife?" presupposes "You have beaten your wife," which in turn presupposes "You have a wife." If you are not married or if you are married and have never beaten your wife, the presuppositions for asking the question have not been met and the act of questioning has not been properly consummated. If you attempt to answer, you implicitly agree that the presuppositions of the question are true and accept the charge of being a wife beater. If you believe the question was asked not as a true question but solely in the hope that you will accept the presuppositions, there is nothing you can do but deny them.

It is not always necessary to use a performative verb in order to indicate the illocutionary force of a sentence. There are syntactic signals: declarative sentences can be used to make assertions, imperative sentences to issue commands or make requests for action, interrogative sentences to ask questions or make requests for information. "It's raining" will normally have the illocutionary force of "I assert that it's raining"; "Stand still" has the force of "I

Ambiguity

Something is ambiguous if it can be interpreted in two or more ways. A two-dimensional picture is ambiguous, for example, if it can be seen as representing two or more three-dimensional scenes. An ambiguous picture is really two or more pictures at the same time.

The drawings below illustrate visual ambiguity. The Necker cube (left), a classic example of reversal of perspective, was discovered by the 18th-century mineralogist L. A. Necker, who noticed such reversals in his drawings of crystals. In the Necker cube shown the corner marked with a dot seems to switch from a front wall to a back wall. The Schröder stairs (center), first published in 1858 by H. Schröder, also illustrate perspective reversal. If the viewer considers the wall marked with a star as part of the background, the stairs seem to go up to the left. When the perspective is reversed, the wall is part of the foreground, and the viewer sees the underside of the stairs going down to the right. The patterns of lines called a blivet (right) may be seen as an object with either three cylindrical prongs or two rectangular ones. It is impossible to conclude which view of these ambiguous drawings is correct, because each perception is equally true.

Out of context, an ambiguous sentence, like an ambiguous drawing, can be interpreted as expressing two or more ideas. A sentence like "The police must stop drinking after midnight" can seem to flip back and forth between its two interpretations. As in the case of ambiguous pictures, it is difficult to keep both meanings in mind at the same time.

At least three kinds of ambiguous sentences should be distinguished:

(1) Lexical ambiguity is illustrated by "The sailors enjoyed the port," where "port" can be understood as either harbor or wine. Sometimes one interpretation is much more salient than the other. In garden-path jokes, a reversal of salience is used to achieve a humorous effect: "I was going to take the plane to Boston, but it was too heavy" plays on two meanings of "take": first "catch," then "carry."

(2) Phrasal ambiguity occurs when a sentence can be parsed in more than one way. "They are visiting relatives," for example, can be parsed as "They (are visiting) relatives" or as "They are (visiting relatives)." "Visiting" is a verb in one interpretation and an adjective in the other. When such sentences are spoken, the intended phrasal grouping can be indicated by appropriate stress and intonation.

(3) Derivational ambiguity is illustrated by sentences like "Visiting relatives can be a nuisance," where both interpretations have the same phrasal grouping and the intended meaning cannot be indicated by special stress or intonation. One version is derived transformationally from an underlying structure that might have become "A visit to relatives can be a nuisance" and the other from one that might have become "Relatives who are visiting can be a nuisance."

Experiments that measured the time it took for readers to see a second meaning have shown that, on the average, lexical ambiguities are easier to see than phrasal ambiguities, which are easier than derivational ambiguities. Those results were obtained in an unnatural situation, however. When ambiguous sentences occur in ordinary conversation, the context nearly always determines which meaning the speaker intended, so the fact that the same sentence could have been used with a different meaning in a different context is irrelevant and usually unnoticed.

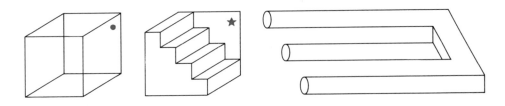

order (request) you to stand still"; "Is it raining?" has the force of "I ask you to tell me whether it's raining."

Requests, either for action or information, are essential for cooperation among members of a group, and the possibility of more-effective cooperation is presumably why language evolved. It is probably no accident, therefore, that we have a variety of ways of using language to make requests, ways that are finely tuned to the personal relation between requester and requestee.

What does a request presuppose? In order for a speech act to count as an attempt by the speaker to get the hearer to do x, (1) the hearer must be able to do x and the speaker must believe that the hearer is able to do x, (2) it must not be obvious that x would get done anyway in the normal course of events and (3) the speaker must want x done and want the hearer to do it. Whether or not the request will be successfully consummated depends on the hearer's willingness to do x, but willingness to comply is not presupposed; you can request someone to do something even when you are reasonably sure of being refused.

If a speaker believes all these conditions are met, he can say "I request that you do x" or, more directly, "Do x," using the imperative mode. If the hearer wishes to refuse the request, he can simply say "No," but usually he will give a reason for refusing. The reason will often be that one of the presuppositions is not met: (1) "I can't," (2) "Mary is taking care of it" or (3) "You don't really want me to."

Because people do not like to have a request refused, they usually lay the groundwork before making it: (1) "Can you do x?" or (2) "x isn't getting done" or (3) "I wish that x were done." Interpreted literally, none of these is a request for the hearer to do x, yet the hearer can recognize that the presuppositions for a request are being established and can respond to the question or assertion as if it were the request. Indirect requests are more comfortable for both parties; the matter can be disposed of without risking the embarrassment of a direct refusal.

When we examine conversational interactions in detail, therefore, we see that sentences that would be ambiguous out of context are really not ambiguous at all but are interpreted immediately in terms of the cooperative conventions of conversational interaction. Perhaps the way to say it is if you are interested in sentences, you will use one definition of ambiguity, but if you are interested in conversations, you will use a different definition. Each definition can be helpful in revealing processes that occur at different levels of information processing, but it would be wrong to confuse them. Ambiguous sentences are very common. Genuinely ambiguous conversational interactions are remarkably rare, and it is even rarer for any serious ambiguity to go uncorrected for long.

People do misspeak, of course. In the vast majority of

Understanding Rules

Some philosophers have argued that we understand the meaning of a (declarative) sentence if we understand the conditions under which it would be true. By this criterion, most of us understand a great deal less than we think we do.

Peter C. Wason, a psychologist at the University of London, showed people four cards:

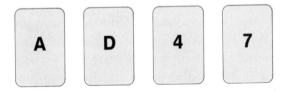

From previous experience they knew that every card had a letter written on one side and a number written on the other side. Wason then gave them this rule about these four cards:

Rule: If a card has a vowel on one side, it has an even number on the other side.

"Your task," he told them, "is to say which of the cards you need to turn over in order to find out whether the rule is true or false."

Most people answered "A and 4" or "Only A."

Both answers are wrong. The correct answer is A and 7. The only cards that test the rule are those that could falsify it. Wason's results have been replicated many times in a variety of experiments designed to test alternative hypotheses as to why this apparently simple rule is so hard to understand correctly.

Few people understand such sentences by valid logical reasoning. Instead, they find the problem baffling and choose A and 4 simply because the rule mentions vowels and even numbers. Having made a choice, they search for reasons to justify it. They say, for example, that they have to test 4 to ensure that the reverse is a vowel or that they don't have to test 7, because the result would be inconclusive or because the rule doesn't say anything about odd numbers. They sometimes give an incorrect rationalization for a correct choice. For someone untrained in logic, any reason that seems to justify a conclusion already reached is as good as any other.

Do Wason's results mean such rules are very difficult to understand? Or do they mean we can understand a sentence without knowing the conditions under which it would be true? Many psychologists think Wason's results mean that different levels of understanding must be distinguished, some of them much deeper than others.

cases, speakers correct their own mistakes, usually during the same conversational turn in which the mistake occurred. If a mistake is not corrected, the hearer may pause before replying, which gives the speaker a second opportunity to correct himself. And if the hearer does not correct the mistake during his turn, the person who made the mistake has a third chance on his following turn. That is to say, the conventions of turn taking give three opportunities for self-correction to only one opportunity for other-correction. But even when a chance for other-correction occurs, the other person seldom takes advantage of it: if the other person understood what the speaker intended to say, he does not need to correct it; if he did not understand what the speaker intended, he is not able to correct it. The upshot is a strong preference for self-correction—which may explain why children get so little reliable information from adults about the syntactic errors they make. Conversations are not viewed as occasions for teaching grammar but as occasions for cooperative social interaction.

The value of cooperation in accomplishing tasks of importance to individuals and groups is fairly obvious, although the way we actually use language to establish cooperation is often subtle and indirect. Less obvious, perhaps, is the kind of cooperation required to hold a conversation at all. Not only must conversationalists cooperate in turn taking but speakers must wish to be understood; they must cooperate by making their contributions informative and germane to the hearer's interests, by anticipating the hearer's problems with anaphora and deixis and by laying the groundwork for what they want to say. And hearers must wish to understand; they must cooperate by drawing all the inferences that follow, not just from what the speaker says but also from the speaker's presumed wish to be understood.

It is fortunate, therefore, that we have inherited a cooperative mentality. It is important that we be able to understand each other, and understanding what another person says is a kind of problem solving. The speaker sets the problem, and it must be both solvable and worth solving. Without cooperation in both setting and solving, language would be useless as a means of communication.

12

Language and Thought

Ever since Plato said that thought is the soul's discourse with itself, philosophers and psychologists have debated the relation between language and thought. Plato's remark suggests they are identical, a view that has been echoed in the 20th century by behaviorists who define thought as subvocal speech. Others are more reluctant to confuse talking with thinking. Not only do people often speak before they think but much thinking is language free: apes seem to think (even without sign language), aphasic patients with severely impaired speech do not have comparably impaired intelligence and many great thinkers have agreed with Einstein's claim that he did not use words when he was doing his best thinking.

Instead of asking how language contributes to thought, therefore, let us focus on how thought contributes to language. And instead of asking how people's thoughts determine what they say, let us consider the kind of problem solving that hearers must do in order to understand what is said—then we will at least know what linguistic problem the hearer is thinking about.

As language users, we solve the hearer's problem so frequently and automatically that we are apt to underestimate how much thinking it entails. We have to listen to speakers in a very literal frame of mind in order to recognize how much they expect a listener to contribute. Even when people say what they mean (which is less often than they imagine), they leave so much unsaid that only an intellectual gymnast can leap from one sentence to the next.

Logic was once believed to be the language of thought. That was before we understood how short the leaps are that logic can negotiate. Strictly speaking, formal logic cannot even go from "Fido is a poodle" to "Fido is a dog," because the relation between these sentences depends on their meaning, not their form. Logic can go from "All poodles are dogs and Fido is a poodle" to "Fido is a dog," but it makes for dull conversation.

If someone were to say "This friend of mine has a tabby and a poodle, and the dog really loves the cat," we would understand immediately that "the dog" is an anaphor for the antecedent "a poodle," and that "the cat" is an anaphor for the antecedent "a tabby" and not the other way round. What logic tells us is that we did not understand this sentence as immediately as we thought we did, because our understanding must be mediated by appeal to the unspoken information that all poodles are dogs and all tabbies are cats.

People do not ordinarily say "Poodles are dogs," because they assume that anybody who speaks English already knows that poodles are dogs. A basic maxim of conversational cooperation is, Do not tell people what they already know. It might not violate the maxim to tell a child or a foreigner that poodles are dogs, but among English-speaking adults this information is taken for granted.

Like all maxims, the maxim to be informative can be violated. It can be violated inadvertently if we do not know that someone already knows what we are telling him, or it can be violated deliberately, as it is when we remind someone of something he knows but has overlooked for the moment:

A: I just bought a French poodle.

B: What you need is a dog that'll protect you.

A: Well, poodles are dogs.

Violations of the maxim to be informative have a special conversational status. In this case, B recognizes both that A has violated the maxim and that A knows it, but B also believes that A is continuing the conversation and therefore that A trusts B to understand why A has violated the maxim. Instead of taking offense at the violation, therefore, B can interpret it as an indirect way of saying "The poodle will protect me." That is to say, B is expected to recognize that A has accepted B's premise and added another, giving "Poodles are dogs and dogs will protect you," from which B should draw the logical conclusion.

Because this explanation makes a simple matter look difficult, we should not regard it as a psychological reconstruction of the thought processes of either participant in the conversation but as a demonstration that their thought processes, whatever they may in fact consist of, are logically defensible. This demonstration is not trivial, for if our conversational inferences were logically indefensible, conversation could not serve its social purpose.

Consider another example, this one requiring a longer leap:

A: I've got a headache. Do you have any aspirin?

B: There's a store around the corner.

On the face of it "Do you have any aspirin?" is a request for information, but we have already seen how such questions are used to make indirect requests for action. B, however, responds by giving information. From B's response, A understands that B does not have any aspirin, but, from general (and therefore unspoken) knowledge that aspirin is sold in stores, A also understands that B is suggesting a plan of action for getting some. More precisely, A assumes that B is observing another basic conversational maxim: Make what you say relevant. The location of a store is relevant to a need for aspirin only if the store sells aspirin and if it is open. In order to leap the gap from A's request to B's response, therefore, A must assume that B thinks the store sells aspirin and is open.

Note that logic needs considerable help here. There is no way that "A needs aspirin and there is a store around the corner" can logically imply either "The store around the corner sells aspirin" or "The store around the corner is open." The relation between these sentences is not one of logical implication or entailment, but one of presumption, suggestion or plausibility—philosophers, following Paul H. Grice of the University of California at Berkeley, call it a conversational implicature, rather than a logical implication. Only on the assumption that B is being cooperative can A assume what B says is relevant to the request, and only on the assumption that it is relevant can A assume the store sells aspirin and is open.

Before A sets out to the store to buy aspirin, there is still another basic conversational maxim that A must assume B observed: Be truthful. This maxim is probably the most important of all. Recall that the hearer's problem is to infer what the speaker has in mind from evidence provided by what the speaker says. The hearer must assume, therefore, that what the speaker says is true about whatever the speaker has in mind, because otherwise the hearer would have no evidence to work from. Moreover, the speaker knows that the listener must make this assumption and that it can be exploited. The speaker can tell a deliberate lie. But lying can only succeed because speakers overwhelmingly observe the maxim to be truthful. And speakers observe the maxim to be truthful because otherwise the whole cooperative basis for linguistic communication would collapse—hearers would have no reliable evidence from which to infer speaker's meanings.

When people tell lies they know their hearers will recognize, we do not ordinarily say they are lying. If someone says of another person, "John is a pig," the hearer is expected to recognize that this is false. The hearer knows, moreover, that the speaker knows the hearer will recognize the falsehood of a literal interpretation, and therefore, the hearer knows that the speaker expects the hearer to search for a figurative interpretation—for example, "John has some properties that are characteristic of pigs"—in order to preserve the hearer's fundamental assumption that whatever a cooperative speaker says can be taken as valid evidence about the speaker's state of mind. Transparent falsehoods like "John is a pig" are called metaphors. The most elaborate falsehoods are fictional stories and novels, where the assumption must be "true in the story," not "true in fact."

Conversational implicatures require a hearer to bring considerable information to bear and to use it in some relatively subtle reasoning. This additional information processing takes additional time. In a simple psychological experiment people were asked to read a pair of sentences, one after the other, and to signal when they comprehended them; the time from presentation to comprehension was recorded. Two kinds of pairs were used. One kind involved simple anaphora:

John ordered some beer. The beer was warm.

The other required the comprehension of an implicature:

John ordered some lunch. The beer was warm.

In the first, "the beer" is an anaphor for "some beer" in the preceding sentence. In the second, there is no antecedent for "the beer"; it is implicated that John ordered beer with his lunch. Finding implicatures to leap the gaps between these sentences takes a significant amount of additional time. The experiment illustrates one way the thought processes must actively support our use of language.

If a conversation is to succeed, each participant must cooperate by observing the maxims to be intelligible, truthful, relevant and informative. When a speaker violates these maxims, the hearer must first decide whether the speaker is being uncooperative—whether he is refusing to pursue the subject, being insulting, breaking off the conversation or what. If the hearer decides that the speaker has not broken the conversationalists' cooperative contract, the hearer must infer the speaker's meaning, not from what is said or implied but from what is conversationally implicated. The conversational maxims can be violated to achieve special effects, but the price is extra work for the hearer.

The reason a speaker should be intelligible is obvious, and we have already considered why a speaker should be truthful. The reasons for being relevant and informative are best considered together.

To be informative, a speaker must tell you something you do not already know. Because there are many things you do not know, this maxim places few constraints on what a speaker might contribute. The maxim to be relevant provides the missing constraints. In order to be relevant, a speaker must relate new information to something you already know. Taken together, the two maxims might be stated, Introduce new information by relating it to familiar information.

We have already encountered linguistic phenomena that illustrate our conformity to this compound maxim, but it may be helpful to review them from this new perspective:

Contrastive Stress. Stress is used to mark new information; familiar information is normally unstressed. If you ask "Who hit John?" the reply "MARY hit John" stresses the information that is unfamiliar and relates it to something your question indicates you already know. If you ask "Whom did Mary hit?" the reply is "Mary hit JOHN," and again the stress is for the same reason.

Turn Taking. In an adjacent pair of linked conversational turns, only new information need be given in the second turn: "Who hit John?" "Mary"; "Whom did Mary hit?" "John." The relation of the new information to familiar information is given by the conventions of turn taking.

Anaphora. Information given contextually—either in preceding conversation or in the current situation—is taken to be familiar and can serve as the antecedent for anaphoric reference. For example, the indefinite article signals a new referent; the definite article generally signals a referent already known. Thus, "I saw a boy and a girl, and a girl was running" is about two girls, but "I saw a boy and a girl, and the girl was running" is about one girl. Pronominalization also signals reference to information given antecedently: "I saw a girl and she was running."

Presupposition. New information is asserted; familiar information is presupposed. If you say "Both of John's children are asleep," you presuppose that your listener knows John has two children, and you assert the new information that they are asleep. If, on the other hand, you say "Both of the sleeping children are John's," you presuppose that your listener knows two children are sleeping and assert the new information that they are John's.

Definition. New words can be defined in terms of familiar words. "A bachelor is a man who has never been married" assumes that the hearer already knows "man" and "married." The definition consists of an assignment to a familiar semantic category, "A bachelor is a man," followed by a restrictive relative clause, "who has never been married," that differentiates this member from all other members of the category. If a child asks what a zebra is, an adult may answer that it is a horse with stripes, thus assuming that the child knows what horses are. If in some part of the world there are children who know about zebras and ask about horses, they are probably told that horses are zebras without stripes.

Clearly, our proclivity for introducing new information by relating it to old information has important consequences for the way we use language. When we ask why this should be so, the answer is reasonably obvious. It reflects one way our minds work—one way we perceive, learn and think about ourselves and the world that we live in. We think inductively.

You encounter some object you have never seen before and call it a chair. In order to do that, you must make a judgment that this new thing is similar to a class of familiar things you have learned to call "chairs." Once you have assigned it to that class, you assume you can do anything with this new object that you have learned to do with familiar objects in the same category. Your subsequent behavior depends on how you relate information about this new object to your old information about similar objects.

You encounter a problem you have never solved before and solve it by reducing it to two other problems you do know how to solve: in order to get from *a* to *b*, first solve the familiar problem of getting from *a* to *x*, then solve the familiar problem of getting from *x* to *b*. You think about new problems by trying to relate them to problems you already understand.

You encounter a legal problem and go to a lawyer. The practice of law is based on the assumption that every new legal conflict is similar to some previous conflict that has already been decided. Your lawyer's job is to argue which precedent applies to your case. Society runs on precedent, on the assumption that new situations can be related to familiar situations.

In short, the human mind is constantly on the alert for analogies that will relate new experience to something already known and familiar. Reasoning by analogy is probably our most fruitful source of hypotheses about any intellectual problem. We know, of course, that there are false analogies, but we would have little to prove or disprove if analogy did not yield hypotheses for logic and experiment to test. It is hardly surprising, therefore, that we shape our use of language to conform to this ubiquitous way of thinking. It has the effect of imposing order and direction on the way we talk.

Consider statements of similitude. Most people assume that similarity is a symmetrical relation, that if a is like b, then b is also like a. But people are usually more familiar with one member than with the other. If they are more familiar with b, they will say "a is like b," but if they are more familiar with a, they will say "b is like a." If we use N to represent the new or less familiar term and o to represent the old or more familiar term, and if SIM stands for such copulas of similitude as "is like," "resembles" and "is similar to," then the general formula for statements of similitude is: SIM(N, O), or "N is similar to o."

For example, when 69 people were asked whether they preferred to say "North Korea is similar to China" or to say "China is similar to North Korea," 66 of them selected "North Korea is similar to China," because China is the more prominent of the two—they were familiar with more features of China than of North Korea, and they preferred SIM(N, O) to SIM(O, N). When another group was asked to rate the degree of similarity of countries on a 20-point scale, they consistently assigned higher ratings to comparisons phrased as SIM(N, O) than to comparisons phrased as SIM(O, N).

When someone says "John's wife is like his mother," it is a simple statement of similitude; if you know John's mother, the statement tells you something about his wife. "John's wife is like his umbrella," however, requires you to do some thinking. It seems to have violated the maxim to be intelligible, but if you believe the speaker is still cooperating in the conversation, you must figure out the implicature. From the general form of statements of similitude you know that the implicature must have the following form: some properties P of John's wife are also properties of John's umbrella, or SIM(P(wife), P(umbrella)). From the directional character of such statements you also know that it tells you something about John's wife, not his umbrella ("John's umbrella is like his wife" would have a very different meaning); from the choice of "is like" rather than "resembles" you know that the similarity is probably one of function, not appearance. You have, in short, considerable information available to think about. What is the function of an umbrella? It protects you from the rain. You cannot transfer this function directly to John's wife, however, unless you are prepared to believe that John holds his wife over his head when he goes out in the rain. On grounds of plausibility you will probably decide that the speaker meant that the way John uses his wife to protect himself from something is similar to the way he uses his umbrella to protect himself from the rain. The speaker has told you something new about John's relation to his wife by relating it to something you already knew about umbrellas.

Not all similes are as banal as that example. In "The Love Song of J. Alfred Prufrock," T. S. Eliot has the phrase "When the evening is spread out against the sky/Like a patient etherised upon a table." A person reading this for the first time will probably never before have connected evening skies and etherized patients, but once he has worked it through—once he has found those properties of etherized patients that can be transferred to evening skies—he may never see the stillness of evening in the same way again. There is no apparent limit to the power of conveying new ideas by relating them to something familiar.

The problem posed by "John's wife is like his umbrella" is almost too simple to be interesting, but we can make it more challenging by turning it into a metaphor: "John's wife is his umbrella." Then the hearer must perform an extra mental step: he must recover the simile on which the metaphor is based and then proceed as before. In this case, it is not difficult to recover the simile, but some metaphors are more complicated.

Consider another line from "The Love Song of J. Alfred Prufrock": "The yellow fog that rubs its back upon the window-panes." The problem, obviously, is that fog does not have a back. The maxims to be intelligible and truthful seem to have been violated, but because the violation is deliberate, we must search for the implicature. Eliot's line is a metaphor, so the implicature will have the form of a simile: some property of fog is like back-rubbing by something, or SIM(P(fog), BACK-RUBS(something)). What rubs its back on things? A cat. What property of fog might be like a cat rubbing its back? Swirling, perhaps. If we substitute "cat" for "something" and "swirls" for "P," the reconstructed simile would be "The yellow fog that swirls upon the window-panes like a cat rubbing its back." Eliot has given us a new idea about fog by relating it to something familiar about cats.

So far, I have assumed that the task of understanding a metaphor is one of reinterpreting the words to make them fit something we already know or believe about the world. This assumption is all right, as far as it goes, but there is another way to look at metaphor. If Eliot meant that fog swirls upon the windowpanes like a cat rubbing its back, why didn't he say so? Why did he say something obviously false and set his reader the apparently unnecessary task of unscrambling what he really meant? The practical mind grows impatient with such verbal play. Yet other readers seem to take pleasure in it. Why?

The alternative view of metaphor would hold that Eliot meant exactly what he said. In that case, the task of understanding a metaphor is one of reinterpreting what you know or believe about the world in order to make it fit the words. That is to say, Eliot's line invites you to imagine, however briefly, a world in which fogs are alive and rub their backs like cats. It challenges your pedestrian assumptions about reality.

Which view of metaphor is correct? Both are. Eliot meant both that fog is like a cat and that fog is a cat; he challenged both our ability to solve the implicature and our ability to imagine something new and different. But the two meanings are incompatible: "Fog is like a cat" may be true, but "Fog is a cat" is surely false. Hence, there is a tension between the two meanings, a tension we feel compelled to resolve somehow. The reduction of that tension is the source of our aesthetic enjoyment.

This pursuit of the thought processes involved in solving the puzzles set by speakers seems to have led us into esoterica. Poetry is a special use of language. A prudent scientist should probably confine his analyses to more mundane linguistic phenomena. In this case, however, the poet is merely exploiting a linguistic resource that colors our most ordinary speech.

Our vocabulary is crammed with dead metaphors: leg of a table, a cold person, father of his country, ship of state, leaf of a book, fiery temper, see the idea, head of cabbage and so on and on. Metaphor is one of the basic mechanisms underlying the growth and change of languages. For example, the English word "crane" originally referred only to birds, then became a way of lifting the head as a crane does and finally became any kind of hoisting device. When we need a new term for something, we frequently choose an old term for something similar and give it a new sense. Because the new thing is related by similarity to something familiar, we find it easier to remember its name.

Languages are not static. They grow and change to suit the needs of those who speak them. But just as the mutant is never totally different from its parent, so the new linguistic forms are never totally different from the old. Language is the servant of man, and man relies on the old to make the new intelligible.

We have not considered all the ways language and thought are related, but perhaps this discussion is enough to suggest the complexity of their relations. The problems involved are critically important for any scientific theory of the human mind, for human language is surely our richest source of evidence about the nature of human thought.

Guide to Further Reading

A First Language: The Early Stages. Roger William Brown. Harvard University Press, Cambridge, Massachusetts, 1973. Combines a scholarly review of studies of early child language with a detailed report of the author's own research.

Syntactic Structures. Noam Chomsky. Mouton Publishers, The Hague, 1957. A little book that initiated a major revolution in theoretical linguistics.

Psychology and Language: An Introduction to Psycholinguistics. Herbert H. Clark and Eve V. Clark. Harcourt Brace Jovanovich, Inc., New York, 1977. A good introduction to psycholinguistics. The extensive bibliography can lead readers as deeply as they care to go into any part of the field.

Syntax. Peter W. Culicover. Academic Press, Inc., New York, 1976. A challenging introductory text in the formal syntax of language, with special treatment of the relation between linguistic theory and the theory of language acquisition.

The Speech Chain: The Physics and Biology of Spoken Language. Peter B. Denes and Elliot N. Pinson. Anchor Press/Doubleday, Garden City, New York, 1973. A very readable survey of scientific approaches to the study of the spoken message at all stages of its progress from the speaker to the hearer.

The Integrated Mind. Michael S. Gazzaniga and Joseph E. LeDoux. Plenum Publishing Corporation, New York, 1978. An authoritative review and evaluation of recent studies of patients whose two hemispheres of the brain have been disconnected. Because speech functions are lateralized, the separation of the hemispheres in these patients offers unusual insights into the neurological bases of language.

Linguistic Theory and Psychological Reality. Edited by Morris Halle, Joan Bresnan and George A. Miller. The MIT Press, Cambridge, Massachusetts, 1978. A collaborative effort by psychologists and linguists to formulate a theory of language adequate for both sciences.

Biological Foundations of Language. Eric H. Lenneberg. John Wiley & Sons, Inc., New York, 1967. A pioneering (and sometimes heavy) statement of the case for a biological basis of the human capacity for language, with detailed evidence for evolutionary specializations.

On the Origins of Language: An Introduction to the Evolution of Human Speech. Philip Lieberman. The Macmillan Publishing Company, Inc., 1975. Combines an excellent introduction to speech science with an interesting discussion of human evolution and of attempts to reconstruct the vocal tract of early man.

Communication, Language, and Meaning: Psychological Perspectives. Edited by George A. Miller. Basic Books, Inc., Publishers, New York, 1973. A collection of 25 essays in which leading authorities explain their ideas and research to a popular audience.

Spontaneous Apprentices: Children and Language. George A. Miller. The Seabury Press, Inc., New York, 1977. Describes the author's experiences while studying the vocabulary development of young children.

Why Chimps Can Read. Anne J. Premack. Harper & Row, Publishers, Inc., New York, 1976. A brief, readable account of communication between people and chimpanzees.

Speech Acts: An Essay in the Philosophy of Language. John R. Searle. Cambridge University Press, London, 1969. A philosopher's exposition of the theory that you not only say something, you also do something when you speak.

The Origin and Diversification of Language. Morris Swadesh, edited by Joel Sherzer. Aldine-Atherton, Inc., Chicago, 1971. This book, published posthumously, summarizes the conclusions reached after years of study by one of America's greatest authorities on the linguistic prehistory of mankind.

Language Acquisition. Jill G. de Villiers and Peter A. de Villiers. Harvard University Press, Cambridge, Massachusetts, 1978. A thorough and lively review of the current state of research into the processes whereby children come to master their native tongue; the review covers syntactic, semantic and pragmatic aspects of that developmental process.

Syntax, Semantics, and Speech. W. A. Woods in Speech Recognition, edited by D. Raj Reddy. Academic Press, Inc., New York, 1975. An excellent discussion by a leader in computational linguistics about how computers process language.

Index

Page numbers in *italics* refer to illustrations.